Coming Home

Awakening through the stillness
into the living light

Fi Sutherland

Publisher: The ISIS School of Holistic Health

Published in the United Kingdom by:
The ISIS School of Holistic Health
www.theisisschoolofholistichealth.com

The author acknowledges permission to reprint material from
The ISIS School of Holistic Health's Newsletters.
And use teaching material from the School's meditation workshops.
The exercise in Chapter 17, A Practice of Unconditional Love, is based on a meditation in Fotoula Adrimi's book *The Golden Book of Wisdom: Ancient Spirituality and Shamanism for Modern Times (copyright © 2018)*. It is used with permission from Fotoula Adrimi.

Disclaimer
The author of this book does not offer medical advice or advocate the use of any techniques as a form of medical treatment for physical or mental illness without the advise of a physician. The intent of the author is to offer information of a general nature to help the reader in their spiritual journey. In the event you use any of the information or exercises in this book, which is your right, the author and publisher assume no responsibility for any outcomes.

A CIP record of this book is available from the British Library.

First printed 2020

Cover design by Eryn Strachan, Moonwood Arts, www.moonwoodarts.co.uk

Layout and design by Heather Macpherson,
Raspberry Creative Type, www.raspberrycreativetype.com

Author pictures by Graeme Henderson, Instagram: gahenderson365

Published with the help of Indie Authors World, www.indieauthorsworld.com

ISBN 978-1-9996410-2-3 (pbk)
ISBN 978-1-9996410-3-0 (ebook)

To all my teachers,
especially my late parents, Margaret and Bob,
and my brother, Stewart

Contents

Foreword

We are born with a yearning toward the unknown and mysterious, that which is just out of our rational grasp. There we engage with questions about our mortality, purpose, and relationship to all of life that is interwoven with these realms of the unknown. In early cultures, there was deep support for this exploration, celebrating and bowing to the magic of the seasons, the cycles of life and death, and the tangible relationship with the diversity of all of life. When this spiritual aspect of our nature, which we are born with, is not given room in our lives, our lives will often come crashing down during times of upheaval and crisis.

Fi Sutherland's story of her awakening to the mystery of the divine illustrates so beautifully how it can look. After a near-death experience, her life altered irrevocably. She has been following the deep teaching that came through her cracked-open heart and soul for over a decade now. Her apt description of this journey is one "from mind to heart—the sacred heart, and of developing connection within to the Divine Self—the authentic Self." Fi began looking for answers from inside rather than outside, and this has brought her to her abiding connection with all of life and her unique responsibility to it.

In following Fi's story, and the wonderful teaching on how to access our heart and Divine nature, we begin to uncover our own story of wholeness and connection. Fi is one of those who guides us to question our limited reality, and open to our spiritual nature, which is a birthright of all humanity, and all of life.

Meredith Little
Cofounder, School of Lost Borders
Big Pine, California
www.schooloflostborders.org

Preface

In 1995, out of the blue, I had my first wake-up call. One Saturday afternoon, I walked into a cinema in Auckland, New Zealand, as the me I thought I was, and I came out two hours later confused and disorientated. The experience upended my world. Days later, I knew I had to find out about meditation, something I had not been aware of prior to watching the film. Meditation sparked my interest in understanding my mind and myself. I also found myself seeking answers to fundamental questions that I had never before considered, such as, Who am I? Why am I here? In the process, I became passionate about personal and spiritual development.

From that wake-up call in 1995 I have had two defining moments in my spiritual journey. The first was in 2007. After many years of procrastination, denial, and fear, I committed wholeheartedly to follow my spiritual path. I set aside my mind's way of directing my life and chose to be guided by my inner voice and heart. I wanted to put my heart in the driver's seat and make decisions in accordance with its guidance. In 2007, I turned fifty, and I knew there was no turning back. I did not want to live with fear for the rest of my life and ignore my heart's calling.

The second wake-up call was in 2009 when I had a near-death experience whilst on a spiritual pilgrimage in Peru. Emerging from four days in a coma after a reaction to the altitude I awoke as a shining spirit, the authentic Self, with a child's perspective of the world. In this state of being, I was able to experience life from an enlightened perspective, from a place of love, joy, and peace. Although this state gradually left me as I worked with an experienced energy healer to fully integrate back into my body, I learnt more about myself in the process. I could clearly see the difference between the spirited Self and the self who had lived on Earth over five decades.

Now, the experience of the enlightened state is in the cells of my body as cell memory. I carry an inner knowingness that we are much more than our conditioned thinking would have us believe.

Since 1995, I have been devoted to personal development—my own and others'. As a counsellor and life coach, I have worked therapeutically with many people who, like myself, were seeking answers to life issues or looking for a better way to live life. We each walk a unique path. There is no one-size-fits-all in any area of personal work. And yet, we can learn from the stories of others. We can resonate and gain insight and receive confirmation of our own process from another's narrative and perspective. It is in this light that I share with you my journey of awakening, insights from my professional training, and clinical observations.

Even if our journeys to enlightenment are unique, there are four facets of the path that are universal: awareness, initiation, purification, and Divine union. I will guide you through these facets as they pertain to the mind, body, spirit, and heart. The process inspired this book, to help readers benefit from my experiential journey.

Coming Home is relevant for this time as more of us feel an inner calling to live in an authentic and inclusive way. Manifesting these positive intentions and actions individually and collectively, we can step away from our old paradigms and forge a new path to a more salubrious environment for all living beings.

Personal development is not necessarily difficult. We can change surprisingly quickly if we want to, by making different choices, as I explain in this book. We do not need to fix our life before we start. We can start from where we are right now, no matter our age and circumstances. No one is too old to do this work. Age and lack of time are common excuses the mind can use to derail our wish for change.

Personal development is an act of self-empowerment. For me, it begins with self-love and ends with a prayer.

May we listen when our heart speaks,
and be courageous in our choices.
May we live alive in the moment,
and discover our purpose.
May we experience the happiness and joy that we are,
and share our truth, beauty, and gifts with all.

We all deserve to experience the happiness that lies within. It is our birthright.

Acknowledgements

I first started writing this book in 2008 while on a solitary retreat in a small cottage in a Scottish glen. The first three chapters flowed, and then my inspiration stopped. In 2011, I began again and although I finished the book, life events interceded and took me away from the creative process. Then in 2018, the time felt right to revisit the book, and this new incarnation was born. With hindsight I realise the hiatus in writing allowed me to incorporate the immense personal growth and spiritual development that I have experienced since 2011.

In walking this path I have many people to thank for their support.

First, a big thank you to my family, my late mum, Margaret, my late dad, Bob, and my brother, Stewart, who have taught me so much and who gave permission for their stories to be included. I extend gratitude to all my friends for their support, and thanks to those who allowed me to use your anecdotes. I give thanks to my clients. Through the healing relationships I also learnt a great deal about myself and the human condition.

I offer heartfelt gratitude to my friend, teacher, and colleague in The ISIS School of Holistic Health, Fotoula

Adrimi. Thank you for all your support, wisdom, encouragement, and love. Every day, I am grateful that we met in Peru in 2009. Working with you in the school fills my heart with joy. I am blessed to know you.

Thanks also to my wonderful editor, Lisa Thaler, whose expertise elevated the book to a higher level. I am filled with gratitude for your insights, questions, suggestions, and skill, and for our beautiful working relationship. Thank you Eryn Strachan of Moon Wood Arts, who created the stunning cover. Your creative talent and enthusiasm are a joy to be around. Thanks also to Heather Macpherson, of Raspberry Creative Type for designing the book, and a huge thanks to Kim and Sinclair Macleod of Indie Authors World for your help in the publishing process. Kim, you are a godsend to self-publishers; your knowledge and energy are amazing. And a big thank you to Graeme Henderson for the author pictures.

To Emaho who taught me so much, indirectly and directly, thank you. May I always remember your teachings and your generosity. My thanks to the late Dr Jane Robertson-Reick, former director and tutor at the College of Holistic Medicine, Glasgow. It was a gift to have you as my teacher for three years. I learned so much during our talks, and I appreciate the time you took to guide me personally and in my work.

Thank you to Meredith Little, cofounder of the School of Lost Borders, for your beautiful foreword. I am forever grateful for our meetings in the Inyo Mountains and in Death Valley. The way you live and work from your heart is inspiring.

I also want to acknowledge and give thanks to the wise teachers and enlightened beings from the spirit realm who have guided and supported me so gracefully in my spiritual journey. Thank you for your encouragement, patience, and love. I am also grateful for your wisdom and insights that I share throughout the book. My life and this book are richer with your presence.

Exercises

Introduction

To navigate and survive in the world, we create the ego. Functioning like a mask, the ego is our protective shell with which we meet external reality. This is healthy and necessary up to a point—until we believe the mask is all we are. When we realise that there is more to us than the mask, an inner search begins. "Who am I?"

Personal and spiritual development is about seeking the answer to that question by slowly letting the ego mask fall away, step by step. At the same time, we connect with our authentic Self, which supports the inner enquiry. This connection may take us beyond the ego and its worldview into a new and wider understanding of ourselves and life.

Coming Home: Awakening through the Stillness into the Living Light tells the story of my spiritual awakening out of the ingrained behaviour patterns, thinking, and habits that controlled and directed my life for thirty-eight years, until my first wake-up call at a cinema in 1995. Through the book's five sections and twenty-five chapters, I take the reader on a journey of increasing self-awareness and insight activating the mind, body, spirit, and heart. This knowledge, and the practices and exercises included, are based on my personal experience of awakening, my training as a therapeutic counsellor, my clinical observations with clients, and my awareness of others as a meditation and spiritual teacher.

*Awakening is the process of transforming
our acquired conditioned mind-sets
and behaviours, and opening up to
our spiritual nature.*

In Part I The Mask Slips, I begin by retelling the story of my initial wake-up call, which opened the door of my mind and helped me recognise another viewpoint about life. This opening led me to meditation and kick-started my inner journey. Instead of looking outwards for the answer, for the first time, I turned my focus inward. Over the years, with my increased self-awareness, I negotiated life more skilfully. But only on my fiftieth birthday when I committed to follow my heart, did my life take a different turn. This decision drove me deeper into my personal process. It asked for honesty, and invited me to confront my fears and walk the talk. And it culminated in a trip to Peru, a near-death experience (NDE), and another opening—this time, into the enlightened mind. The NDE changed the direction of my life and in time aligned me with my soul's purpose for this lifetime: teaching personal development and spiritual awakening in the ISIS School of Holistic Health.

I also describe what happens to us as babies born on a planet whose current conditions support the development of the ego mind. From the pristine state of our spirit, that of unconditional love, we each go through a socialisation process that favours the mind over the heart and looks to the external world to satisfy our needs. Shaped by what happens to us, we become estranged from our Divine Self. However, this process need not define us. There is a way out.

In Part II Learning New Ways: The Mind, we begin a journey of self-discovery. A key facet of awakening is the development and application of awareness.

Cultivating self-awareness dislodges our conditioning. Without awareness, healthy change is difficult, if not impossible, to attain and hard to sustain. Lacking awareness, we may not recognise the healthy opportunities that life brings us, and continue to choose the old, familiar ways. We also need to act on our awareness, and life will bring us the situations and people, the initiations, that help us apply our awareness. Applying our awareness provides the mind with evidence that there is a different way of doing things and another way of being. It makes our personal journey experiential, creating a magical alchemy for positive change and growth. Initiation is another facet of awakening.

We see how the mind can both help and hinder our path, and how we can benefit by taking time to understand and respect it and form a different relationship with it. We utilise the mind's ability to transform through learning, exercising discernment and orientating to the positive. We counter its limitations by regulating our responses, supporting our authentic Self and owning our mistakes. We rein in the mind to respond anew to life. We take back our power.

In Part III Listening to Inner Wisdom: The Body, I explain how our socially programmed emotions and inherited biology maintain the inner separation and how we can work in a more integrated way to support the authentic Self. I speak about the impact of emotions—particularly anger and

3

fear—on our body. I show how to experience feelings in a more productive and therapeutic way and release suppressed hurt from the body. Purification is the third facet of awakening.

Then, I turn the spotlight on relationships with others, the ways in which another person can mirror or reflect back what we were not aware of about ourselves (shadow side). Finally, I explain how to develop a salutary relationship with our body, how our body gives us feedback about ourselves and others and how we can interpret this body talk. The body plays a crucial role in awakening. When we awaken through our body, our process will be grounded and sustained, and when we trust the body and listen to its wisdom, an illness can be an initiation into a new consciousness.

In Part IV Nourishing the Soul: The Spirit, the journey continues through unearthing our shadow side, and by turning our attention away from the mind and towards the heart. To sustain transformation we engage with practices that foster self-love (hugging and appreciating our body), kindness (offering reassurance to the frightened aspect of ourselves), and gratitude (focussing in our heart centre and saying thank you for all we have).

Seeking to nourish our soul, we explore spiritual practice as a way of revealing the Divine Self. As we experience moments of Divine union, the fourth facet of awakening, our inner foundation grows. Combining spiritual practices with our personal work can advance our soul's evolution. I then focus on one fundamental spiritual practice—meditation. Meditation helps us clear a path to the awakened state. Through meditation we transcend the ego mind, and enter the silence where the enlightened state speaks to us.

As we walk the path towards wholeness, purification continues. Through our personal work and healing interventions past hurts and trauma are released. On this journey, we may realise that we are not alone. Beings from the unseen world may approach us and offer their support.

In Part V Lighting the Path: The Heart, we leave the conditioned path and strengthen our connection to our sacred heart, the enlightened state within. How? We open ourselves to unconditional love and forgiveness. The door into these qualities is acceptance. Through acceptance we can love ourselves more intimately. We can put down our fears and our burdens, and bathe in the weightlessness of inner freedom. As we surrender into the beauty of our inner light, we flow with life.

This inner state of being can direct our life in a healthier and more meaningful way. From this place of connection, we can more easily access our Divine power and wisdom, and understand that life is about serving the we, rather than the me of the ego's individualised approach. Harnessing the power of intention we learn to detach from the external world, bring our energy inside, embody our Divinity, and reclaim our joy and equanimity.

As you engage deeper with the four facets of awakening—awareness, purification, initiation, and Divine union—through your personal work and spiritual practices, your energy vibration increases. This brings you ever closer to the resonance of the awakened state until one day you become that state. You come home.

PART I:

THE MASK SLIPS

Chapter 1

An Unveiling

Jesus said, "If you bring forth what is within you, what you bring forth will save you. If you do not bring forth what is within you, what you do not bring forth will destroy you."[1]

In 2003, what I wanted to bring forth was a book. I thought I would write fiction, so I joined a creative writing course, but discovered that my heart was not in it. Whenever the desire to write resurfaced, I would squash it with a trail of rationalisations. "The world does not need another book." "You've got nothing new to say." "Who would want to read what you write?" "Who do you think you are?"

Sound familiar? When we dare think about, let alone action, a long-standing idea or dream, the mind can quickly reason against it. Yet, my desire to write remained, and suppressing it was quietly and unconsciously, pulling me down.

Then, in 2008, I was on a personal retreat in a small cabin near Balquidder, Scotland, when the idea popped up again: write a book. I sat down and wrote three chapters in two days. The years passed and those chapters remained untouched on my computer until one day, I opened the door once again and sat down to write. This time, I wrote what was in my soul. I now know I was not meant to write fiction, but share my heart's journey of awakening. This book is the result.

The book helped me in many ways, it provided the opportunity for creative expression; asked me to shed self-consciousness and share my stories; required honesty and a deeper comprehension of the awakening process, which fortified my journey and I hope will inform yours, too; and brought what was in me out, which has created so much joy. I let my mask slip. Jesus was right.

I include the above to illustrate a point. The process I have gone through in writing this book is similar to what many of us go through when we want to step out of our comfort zone, even for a little while.

We have dreams. We have things we would like to do. And yet, how many of us action our ideas and live our dreams? Why do we give up our innermost longings, and perhaps trap ourselves in other people's ideas of who we are? Why do we live according to others' expectations for us, such as our parents' wish to follow them into the family profession? Is that what life is about?

No matter how we live our life, when we live in a personally unfulfilling way, our health and happiness suffer if we do not take steps to remedy the situation. It can be a slow death, a half-lived life.

I lived that life. I appeared successful, but the cost of not following my inner dreams was slowly crippling me. In 1990, I left my marriage because it did not bring me joy. It was my first real act of nonconformity. After years of unacknowledged sadness, I felt liberated. My then-husband, parents, and friends were taken aback. I had never expressed my feelings about the marriage to anyone, so strong was my attachment to my upbringing where we did not speak about anything personal.

In 1982, two days after the wedding in Scotland, where my family lived, my partner and I moved to New Zealand. When the marriage ended, I decided to remain there. After a while, my life settled into a familiar pattern of materialism and complacency. I worked, had an active social life, paid the bills and the mortgage, went on the annual holiday. Ironically, I still maintained the outward trappings without nurturing my inner longings. I may have gained some independence, but I still was not thinking too deeply about my life.

Then, one weekend in 1995, I flew from my home in Wellington to Auckland, to visit a work colleague. At some point, she suggested going to the local cinema, and being an avid movie fan, I readily agreed. The film she chose had an enormous effect on me. The title is not relevant. Life brings us to the right place at the right time. And the medium life chose for me was that film at that cinema at that time.

I came out of the cinema feeling dismantled—mentally disorientated and emotionally in turmoil. It was as if an earthquake had rocked my foundation, a foundation that, two hours previously, was secure. Or so I thought.

When I returned to Wellington, the questions continued as did the feelings of disquiet, but also of excitement. Clearly, something deep within me had been shaken, but what? What did any of it mean? I had no answers.

Almost every night after work for the next two weeks, I went to the cinema and watched the same movie. I wanted to understand what was happening to me, and the film was my only reference point. Madness? Perhaps. Needless to say, I did not tell anyone what I was doing. The experience felt too precious to share, and I had no words for what was going on within me.

At the last showing of the movie, I left the cinema with a strong inner sense that there was much more to life than how I was living it and how I understood it. It was as if some part of me, which I had no previous knowledge of, had woken up. For the first time, I realised that I was in charge of my life. I felt happy and set free in a way that surprised me—far more so than after the divorce. As this new realisation emerged within, my first instinct was to look upwards. I lifted my eyes to the sky and felt an inner happiness and a sense of expansion. In that moment, I was no longer alone and separate. I felt part of something much bigger than myself, even though I had no idea what it was, only that it felt good and I was at peace for the first time in a long while.

My whole world had been turned upside down; yet outwardly, nothing had changed. I had a felt sense of knowing something, without consciously knowing what the something was; but somehow, that was OK. All I knew was that a door had opened in me and I was happy. A door can open for any of us at any time. And once the door opens, there is no turning back. Life has brought us the situation to learn from. Can you see that?

Then, out of the blue, an image of the American tennis player Stan Smith, whom I had seen meditating on a television programme when I was fifteen, flashed into my head. Instantly, I knew I had to learn to meditate. In a café later that day, I found a flyer for a free meditation class starting the following day. Coincidence? Something was happening, something different, and I decided to go with it.

Meditation helped me develop self-awareness and it led me to Buddhism. Buddhist psychology taught me to better comprehend my mind and the nature of the human experience. Why aren't we taught about this, and how to find fulfilment, at school?

Over the years, self-awareness has allowed me to make better life choices and gain more self-understanding. My perspectives of life and who I am are continually evolving. Some of my revelations are: my learnt mental and emotional responses have dictated my choices; I am in charge of my life in all ways; and I can live my life differently than others live theirs, than my upbringing and my culture would suggest. Paradoxically, at the time, I was in charge of very little.

Then in 2001, I moved back to Scotland, committed to a new relationship, and changed career. I went to university to study psychology, and undertook a diploma in therapeutic counselling. Motivated by my personal experience, I wanted to help others who were struggling in their life.

After a few years, the new relationship ended badly and sent me into a tailspin. Its severe impact on my mental, emotional, physical, and spiritual health was a huge wake-up call. Although painful, I did much soul-searching to understand what had, and where I had, gone wrong. If I was going to move on and learn from the situation, I needed to take full ownership of the choices I had made. I never wanted to repeat this experience. It was too sore. I had to admit to myself that I could study personal development all I liked, sit on a cushion and meditate, but if I did not action what I knew and keep actioning it, then I would continue to make the same mistakes.

In my personal, academic, and professional life, I immersed myself in the science and practice of self-empowerment. My counselling course and the work I did with clients demonstrated the power of personal growth, and in turn, galvanised my resolve with humility and sincerity. It is said that if you want to learn something, teach it. And so, I started teaching personal development. Life had shown me that I needed to learn about myself and to understand what was driving my choices. At the same time, through my increased awareness, I could help other people.

The life lessons continued, and as I opened myself up step-by-step to the learning that each situation offered, I felt happier and more balanced. However, I was also aware of a deep inner niggle that I had been ignoring. At times, I would experience periods of dissatisfaction and self-loathing, though outwardly, it seemed unwarranted. This was confusing and unsettling to my mind and rattled me emotionally, leading me into bouts of depression and despair. I was haunted by complacency and ennui. Why bother? What's the point? In those moments, I wanted to give up everything, even my life.

Then in 2007, on my fiftieth birthday, I looked in the mirror, and finally faced the question. Are you going to fully acknowledge this inner yearning to grow personally and spiritually? Or, are you going to continue sidestepping the issue, with one foot in everyday life and one on a spiritual path? Are you going to play it safe, or take a leap of faith and go for it?

That day, at fifty, I finally committed to follow my heart and the inner longing—whatever that meant and wherever it took me. If I thought my life and thinking had changed before, I had not seen anything yet. Suddenly, I had found the accelerator pedal. I hit the pause button on teaching to devote more time to self-healing. I trusted that the disruption would ultimately make me a more authentic and compassionate and wiser teacher—able to speak from experience.

I began to listen, follow, and trust my inner guidance about what to do and where to go. I began to allow life to come in and present situations to me rather than believing I should plan out life in advance.

Despite mental consternation and fear, I took risks and opened doors that I never would have seen or thought possible. Miraculously, things began to work out and work out well. I trusted myself, and life was supporting me in that process. My life became much more interesting, and far more diverse and richer. I was in an adventure rather than feeling like a passenger on a bus. As the mask slipped, I was waking up.

Chapter 2

Reborn into Bliss

In 2009, I fulfilled a dream to visit Machu Picchu. I was going to South America for the first time and I was elated. I travelled to Peru with a group on spiritual pilgrimage, but I returned home alone. When most of the group left Peru, I was in a coma, in intensive care in a hospital in Cusco, caused by altitude sickness.

My last conscious memory is at the end of our day in Machu Picchu, boarding the bus with some friends to return to our hotel. I do not even recall finding a seat on the bus. My next memory is waking up in the hospital. No memories have ever returned of my missing time: the three days before the coma and the four days I remained in the coma. I know many people have written books about their near-death experiences (NDE), but I cannot tell you anything about mine. What I can tell you is what happened afterward.

When I woke up from the coma four days later, I did not know I had been with a group. I did not recall Machu Picchu; that memory came back later. On waking up, I had no memories. Coming out of the coma was the most amazing experience I have ever had. I felt as if I had been reborn. It was a birthing, except this time I was born into an adult's body—with the innocent perspective of a newborn.

When I awoke, I realised that I was in a hospital. I knew I was in Peru, although I had no idea where. I knew my name and I knew I was from Scotland, but that was all. I could not answer any more of the doctor's questions. I had no idea how old I was or what day or month or even year it was. I had no conception of what had happened to me, nor did I know if anyone knew where I was. The doctor just nodded and smiled, and so did I.

I had a wisp of disappointment when I looked at my hands and noticed that a ring I had worn for years was not there. But as quickly as that feeling arose, it was gone. It did not matter. Nothing mattered. I had no fear, no worries, no concerns, and no thoughts. Let me say that again: I had no fear, no worries, no concerns, and no thoughts. My mind was completely empty of thoughts. Wow. In all my years of meditation, I had not achieved that—a mind empty and spacious, the meditator's dream. My mind was at peace and so was I. I cannot recall ever before feeling so at ease and untroubled. I looked around, and everything I saw was beautiful. I felt content, completely relaxed, and so very happy. Thich Nhat Hanh said, "Enlightenment, peace, and joy will not be granted by someone else. The well is within us."[1] I had found the well.

Then some friends, who had extended their stay, came into the ward. I was so amazed to see people I knew that I burst out laughing. I felt so blessed and happy to see their faces, and I was so surprised and delighted that they knew where I was and had come to visit me. I felt so much love pouring out from them to me and from me to them. We could not stop smiling and laughing, which was good because thinking and talking were not happening for me. So, we spent most of the visit smiling, nodding, and laughing. And when I was not laughing, I was at rest in this inner state of bliss.

My mind was empty and still. I was still. No thoughts came, nor did it occur to me to think or even to speak. I was in a quiet state of being, with no impetus to do anything other than respond to the basic physical needs of eating and going to the toilet.

Eventually, I realised that if I wanted to think I had to consciously engage my mind, but because the whole experience was new to me I did not know this. I had to learn that I needed to think and then consciously think. I developed a strategy of saying to myself "think," and then it took a moment for my mind to kick in before I could think. (I have used this strategy again as I went through the awakening process described in this book.)

A year later, I met up with two of the tour leaders who had remained in Peru to look after me. They told me that when they asked me a question, the words would hang in the air. I would simply smile. I was a child whose language skills had yet to develop, and it would take some time for the skills to come back fully. This was such a disparate state to be in from my normal way of functioning. In my new state, I was bathed in a sea of calm. I was inner peace. I had no need to communicate and it never occurred to me to speak.

The quieter we are, the closer we get to who we are.

When I was back home, while in a state of lucid dreaming (aware while dreaming), I saw myself as a luminous being sitting in front of a council of nine beings. They were seated in a semicircle facing me, and we were communicating. Later, I discovered that many modern-day spiritual people talk of the Council of Nine. This council is responsible for the evolution of consciousness and life on Earth, and is made up of wise beings of light. In my vision, I saw myself with this same luminosity, even though in real life, I am a simple person from a small village in Scotland. The dream showed me that our human soul has the same radiance as the wisest beings of light in the universe.

Four weeks after I left my home in Scotland, arrived in Peru, fulfilled my dream to see Machu Picchu, and landed in the IC unit in Cusco, I was released from the hospital. A few days later, I returned to Scotland in the same expanded state. My parents met me when I got off the plane and were shocked by my appearance. I had lost a lot of weight and had not been sleeping well, due to a constant state of lucid dreaming and its sensory overload.

Any form of communication continued to be fun. It took me a long time to process people's questions and even longer to respond, as I had forgotten the most basic words and how to speak in sentences. Yet, everyone was kind and caring and patient with me. It was like playing a continuous game of charades, as others worked out what I was trying to say.

I went to my doctor, gave him the large wad of notes from my week's stay at the hospital in Peru, and told him about the coma. He said nothing. He offered to sign me off work for two weeks and said that if I needed more time off, I could come back and see him. That was it. I was a bit stunned but of course said nothing given my inability to communicate at the time.

When I returned to work, I had to relearn my job as a clinical supervisor and coordinator of the therapeutic team in a community health project. Again, my colleagues were so kind and gracious that we ended up laughing most of the time. One of my duties was to chair the monthly team meetings for the therapeutic staff. The first team meeting I held was rather chaotic. I could not follow the agenda. I found the whole process so funny, like a child playing the adult. At one point, I was almost hysterical with laughter, and my colleagues alternated between laughter and consternation. I did not have access to any of the human conditioning. My spirit was focused on a bigger perspective, and I could not comprehend the details of human working life.

I was so happy and felt so loved by everyone and so loving towards all. Our spirit truly is unconditional love. Looking back, I am humbled by how much love people had for me. I could feel the love pouring out of people towards me. It was beautiful to experience and in my open state, I could receive it. My usual barriers that block the connection to myself and to others and to their love and support had vanished. When the conditioning is removed, love flows. Each time we overcome an old behaviour pattern, we allow our inner light to glow a little brighter.

I knew instinctively that this experience had given me enormous gifts even beyond the experience of unconditional love and bliss. I could see the concern on the faces of my family and friends—not surprising, given my physical changes, childlike joy, and memory loss, but I felt no anxiety whatsoever. Instead, I felt immense gratitude.

Life was different from my new perspective. It was much more joyful, freer, funnier, and lighter, and my interactions with others, friends and strangers alike, were just as joyful. Most of all, life flowed. I had no struggles. I was living on the planet without any of the conditioned thoughts, feelings, and judgements that had previously shaped and controlled much of my life. All that remained was love. Love is the essence of who I am and the essence of who you are. Love is the essence of who we all are.

In this state, I was living in love, instead of living with fear. I was present in each moment, and only that moment mattered. I had no thoughts about a past or a future because in that space, neither existed. I had no thoughts to distract me from the preciousness of the moment and the love I was bathed in. I had no plans, no agendas, no desires, no sense of lack or separation, no feelings of being lost or lonely, no need to control anyone or any situation, no expectations, no insecurity and no anger or irritation. I had no labels for myself or others and no image of myself to maintain or live up to. I was a pure spirit in a body, a state normally experienced only by babies or by enlightened teachers.

Although I loved my blissful state, I was also aware that I was ungrounded and energetically unstable. At times, so many emotions were running through me that I did not know if I would burst out laughing or crying, which was disconcerting for those around me. I was in a transition phase between worlds, between the world of spirit and the one of physical matter. Being between the worlds was a gift; however, I had a life on Earth that I felt called to live. So, after the illness and coma, I had to come back into my body and integrate these new experiences with my earthbound reality. I knew I needed help. The next day, my phone rang.

On day two of the Peru pilgrimage on our first excursion to a local sacred site, I had sat on the bus next to a woman named Fotoula Adrimi. We connected instantly. And although she was born in Greece, Fotoula was living in Glasgow, as I did.

I answered the phone, and Fotoula was calling to see how I was. I said I was very good spiritually, but physically, emotionally, and mentally I felt fragmented, as if I was falling apart. I knew I needed energy healing. Spontaneously, I asked Fotoula if she could help me. She said yes.

For the next six months, either weekly or fortnightly, I went to Fotoula for her ISIS energy healing sessions. The work she did was led, session to session, by her healing guides and was specific to my state of being in the moment. At first, I could only cope with short sessions of twenty minutes each. Eventually, my energy bodies became stronger and the sessions lengthened and evolved. As well as ISIS healing, I received shamanic healing from Fotoula, such as soul retrievals (where dissociated parts of the soul due to trauma, as well as coma, are reintegrated) and extractions (of heavier energy that I had picked up from others and the environment).

In slowly coming back into my body, I began to lose my connection with my spiritedness. This was a loss, but I knew I could not function or live long-term in such an ungrounded, fragmented state without serious health and financial repercussions. I needed to be stable on every level to honour the gift I had been given and to consciously learn from it. Through a friend, I later learned of someone who went through a similar experience and did not find the help she needed to integrate back into her body in a healthy way. She had a mental breakdown and ended up in a psychiatric hospital for months, which impacted her and her family for many years. I am so grateful that I received helped from Fotoula and that this was not my experience.

Years later, Fotoula shared with me some insights she had been given by her healing guides about my NDE. Many people in an NDE go through a tunnel into the light where they meet spirit guides and see their life, maybe even have a review of their life up to that point and then are turned back into the tunnel and back into their body. I had gone well past the tunnel into the light and merged with the spiritual Divine light. This is why when I came back, I was so luminous and full of unconditional love. My experience is somewhat unique in that I do not remember what happened to me in those realms. When I came back into the body, my energetic structure had disintegrated as I had travelled so far into the spirit realms. My body was in a process of death and could not hold my spirit, which had become so luminous and expanded. I had a toe in the physical world and the rest of my foot was still in the spirit world.

With support from Fotoula, I gradually reintegrated into my body. As I moved from a pristine state of love (the newborn who awoke in the hospital) back into a state of conditioning and life experiences spanning over fifty years (the world of my adult body), I was aware of what was happening to me. I saw how the environment impacted me mentally, my mind busy with thoughts, and I began feeling the heavier emotions such as anger and sadness. I noticed how my focus shifted outwards, and I no longer laughed as much or had direct contact with the inner state of joy and peace. The enlightened state slowly slipped away.

This experience taught me that my authentic Self is not my mind, my emotions, or my body. In coming back into the bodysuit, I came back into the thought patterns, memories, feelings, and behaviours associated with that armour. But these patterns and memories are not who I am. I am a luminous being of love and light, who consciously chose to come back into this vaguely familiar uniform. I now had an opportunity to learn more about myself and what it meant to be in this physical body. What an incredible experience and what an incredible gift I had been given.

The intention I had made on my fiftieth birthday was truly manifesting. My commitment to follow my heart and my spiritual path strengthened, and focused my lifestyle choices. After returning from overseas travels in 2008 (before I went to Peru in 2009), I was living in my parents' home, believing in my financial lack and denying myself my own space and privacy. I was living a life of compromise. So, one of the first things I did, after I began my healings with Fotoula, was to move out of my parents' house.

I found a beautiful flat in Glasgow, and created a dedicated meditation room. I stopped drinking alcohol, which had been my constant companion for years. At different points in my life, alcohol had been a fun and sometimes not-so-fun way of coming out of my shell, a crutch, a means of distraction, and a coping strategy. I could not imagine life without alcohol. For years, I tried to stop only to drink more, which led to terrible bouts of self-judgement. And then, one day in 2010, I realised I was no longer thinking about or buying booze. My need for alcohol had fallen away, quietly, and has never returned.

I also did not go into the city as much as I had. When I returned from Peru, I did not phone friends to meet for coffee, as I normally would have done. Some friends did not phone me either, and our friendship dropped away. I spent more time with myself inside my lovely flat being still, slowing down, and diving deeper into my inner world. I faced the shadows I had also long avoided that were being brought to the surface by the spiritual practices I was now doing and my healing work with Fotoula.

At the same time, unhealthy family patterns re-emerged. This time, I changed my response to one that was self-respecting rather than following my old way of giving in. A great healing took place in the family dynamics, and our relationships became more honest and loving (chapter 12).

This all happened organically, without plans or thoughts. It was a challenging time for me, but I kept walking through the doors that were opening. A different me was unfolding, and I was making space for this expansion by addressing old issues that felt undermining and did not honour my authentic Self. And as my world continued to change, my relationship with myself improved. I became kinder and more respectful and self-nurturing.

Although in coming back into the bodysuit, I lost much of my wakefulness and freedom, I did not lose it all. I had more joy and much less fear, than pre-Peru. I also had a stronger inner connection to who I truly am, alongside a greater awareness of my conditioned self. The enlightened state was now in my body as cell memory. The experience strengthened my commitment to follow my heart with the intention of returning to the state I experienced immediately after the coma. However, this time my wish is to wake up through my heart and through my body, rather than going out of my body, as in the NDE, so that I can hold and embody the awakened state. In that way, too, I will awaken into the wisdom mind that lies behind the doors of the heart: to awaken as both the adult and the wise child.

#

There are four key aspects to the process of awakening.

First, our progress is gradual, so that we can integrate, understand, embody, and build on the personal and spiritual work we do.

Second, the process is comprehensive; it affects all areas of our life. There is an inner and outer purification process. We move away from toxic energies and relationships and focus on the people, food, and lifestyle that nourishes our growth. We create a home environment that nurtures us.

Third, the practice is contemplative. In times of stillness, we can examine and move away from the old behaviours that trigger negative emotional thoughts and feelings that take us out of the state of happiness. We slowly let go of the old patterns that no longer accord with the new self that is emerging.

Fourth, the knowledge is universally applicable. We apply the lessons and strategies we learn to other situations. In time, we notice that our choices are healthier and more self-respectful.

We are waking up and gradually, our life reflects our inner state of being.

Chapter 3

Finding My Path

I am working to return to the peaceful and heart-connected state of my post-coma experience, while being fully grounded and steady within the body. The deeper I immerse myself in my body, the more whole I feel. Instead of going out to the spirit realms to achieve the Divine connection, I am going deeper into the body, into the cells, and into the Divine Self within.

I was both grateful and inspired by the results of the healing work I received from Fotoula Adrimi. I wanted to learn more about the teachings and healing modality that she had channelled from the enlightened spirit teacher who identifies as ISIS (known in ancient Egypt as the Divine Mother of All Beings). Consequently, in 2010, Fotoula initiated me as a student into the First Gate of Awareness of the Teachings of the Living Light: The Path of ISIS. This is both a healing path for oneself and others and a spiritual path of embodied awakening, incorporating meditations, ceremonies, and rituals. When practised regularly, these teachings invite practitioners to deepen their spiritual journey and facilitate the evolution of their soul.

Throughout my years of personal development and a plethora of workshops and courses, two practices have endured: meditation and the teachings of the Living Light: The Path of ISIS. In the Path, I have been helped enormously by the focused meditation practices that are combined with a download of divine consciousness in the form of high vibrational energy. This access to Divine energy was the missing link in my meditation practice. Before the ISIS teachings, I had been meditating daily for sixteen years, following various forms of Buddhist practices, such as vipassana, metta bhavana, and mindfulness. The ISIS work has brought me inner transformation much quicker and in a more sustained and grounded way than my previous meditation practices had.

In 2012, I was introduced by Fotoula to the Rays of Divine Consciousness, a meditation practice that activates the spiritual twelve-strand DNA and brings the essence of light into the body. I worked with the Rays practices daily for the following six years to help purify the karma carried from this and other lifetimes.

Visiting sacred sites around the world has also helped me purify my karma and unearth aspects of the conditioning that separates me from the awakened state. Since Fotoula and I met in Peru in 2009, we have been on many other spiritual pilgrimages. Sometimes, we toured as part of a group; other times, we travelled just the two of us.

The uncovering of our conditioning can happen spontaneously. In 2014 in Tibet, standing in a nunnery transfixed by the sweet sounds of the nuns' chants, I was suddenly overwhelmed with sadness. As we left the nunnery, I was sobbing. Bhola Nath Banstola, Nepalese shaman and guide, put his arms around me. He held me as my tears continued to flow, releasing the sorrow that had been trapped within me. Afterwards, I felt strong and at peace. Bhola looked into my eyes, and we both knew the work was complete. I had no insight into what I had cleared. Was it a memory from a past life, or simply the release of stuck energy triggered by the grace I experienced in the nunnery? I do not know. I do know the work was done and I moved on, feeling lighter.

These experiences have happened so often that I trust the healing process and continue on. If we are meant to understand their significance, this information will come to us in time; if not, it is of no concern. The most important thing is the purification work is done—old energy is released and our being is cleaner and lighter.

In 2012, I was made redundant when the community health project I worked for lost its government funding. Much to the consternation of my parents and friends, my instinct was to focus wholeheartedly on my personal and spiritual development rather than find other employment. As soon as I made the decision, a door opened for me to travel to China. For the next three years, the travel doors continued to open. I accepted all the opportunities I was given to go on retreats, healing journeys, pilgrimages to sacred sites, and vision quests. (A vision quest is a ceremony where people go out into nature usually for four nights and four days without food, and with a clear intention or question to see how the natural world responds to them, and vice versa.)

At times it was not easy, and yet miracles happened too. For example, I was in Egypt in March 2011, immediately after the Egyptian Revolution, when few tourists were in the country. The guards left us alone, walking away from us and our small group, and we spent hours engaged in ceremonial work inside many of the temples.

In December 2014, as I wrote my letter of intent to participate in the March 2015 Great Ballcourt Death and Dying Vision Fast in Death Valley, California, I realised I had found my soul's purpose. Eight years after making the commitment to follow my heart, I was no longer a seeker. I was walking my life's path as a teacher in the ISIS School of Holistic Health alongside Fotoula. The inner calm that has come through discovering my life purpose has been amazing. In response to my letter of intent, the facilitator Meredith Little wrote, "Finding our life purpose is huge."

Was it my intention to find my life purpose when I took the decision to follow my heart in 2007? Not consciously. But in remaining true to my heart's calling and walking through the doors that life presented, I discovered what I am here to do. Step by step, door by door, life and my heart aligned me with my golden path, the path my soul had chosen to live before birth. By releasing my mind's approach to life and following my heart, I found my path. As Joseph Campbell advocates, "We must be willing to get rid of the life we've planned, so as to have the life that is waiting for us."[1]

Finding my path has given my life meaning. In order to stay on my path, I know the inner work must continue. What my soul ultimately seeks is to end the internal egoic state of separation and enter the state of Divine union. My soul yearns to awaken into its authentic essence and so fulfil its inner purpose of luminosity.

#

These first three chapters give an overview of my personal journey. In the following two chapters I confront the nitty-gritty of social conditioning. I share my insights, strategies, and teachings to help you recognise and navigate its influence.

Chapter 4

Socialisation and Conformity

When we incarnate on Earth we are born onto a planet that has well established cultures, traditions, belief systems, and normative behaviours. No matter where we were born or who we are, we will all come under the influence of social conventions to some extent. They are pervasive and influence not only how we live, but also who we think we are. Many of us are so swept up in the socialisation process that we remain unaware that it controls our thoughts, feelings, and behaviour. We act from old habits, ours and our ancestors, unconscious of their capacity to distance us from experiencing the aliveness of life and the truth of our being.

> Born Originals, how comes it to pass that we
> die Copies?[1] —Edward Young, English poet

My earliest traumatic memory is about fear and humiliation and the impotent desire to flee. I am five years old. It is the first day of school, and I am standing with all the other five-year-olds from the village in front of the class. We are the new primary one. The primary two kids are already seated, watching us. I am crying. My body is shaking and I feel scared. Then I hear one of the primary two boys saying, "It's Crybaby Sutherland again," and everyone starts laughing. I want to run away, but I can't. I stay, frozen with embarrassment and shame.

Unbeknownst to me, the trauma of this and similar childhood incidents impacted me for years and altered my behaviour. In my teens, I was so unhappy that I often thought of killing myself, but I was too frightened to actually do it. The only thing I did was to drink Mum's perfume on Sunday nights to make myself ill, so that I would not have to go to school the next day. It tasted so awful, I could not swallow it. At the time, nothing in life seemed to make sense or give me joy, and I disliked the constant pressure that I felt in school to do well, especially in exams, and at home, to be the good girl. Compounded by being a perfectionist and high achiever, the pressure I put on myself was crippling me inwardly, even though outwardly, I acted as if all was well.

Looking back, I think what saved me from imploding was sport. I could release my pent-up energy through volleyball. Training and playing became a positive outlet for my anger and frustration, as well as a major distraction from my dissatisfaction and confusion with life. I loved the game, and being part of a team counteracted the sense of isolation and separateness that I felt. Thus, volleyball became my raison d'être throughout high school and into adulthood. In 1986, when I hurt my back through weight training and stopped playing, I realised just how much volleyball and all the fitness workouts I did had been offsetting my unhappiness. With no sport to deflect my attention, I could no longer deny how despondent I felt in my life and in my marriage—even though it took me another four years to pluck up the courage to leave.

I could see how early traumas and the resultant depressed state coupled with social pressure to excel, were shored up by athletic skill. It was all a cover, albeit useful.

The Socialisation Process

We are born into this world in a perfect state of being, a state of wholeness, fully connected to the truth of who we are. We are pure consciousness, with no anger, fear, hatred, self-doubt, or any sense of unworthiness and insecurity. This is the state I awoke into after my coma. Although we are pristine, the world we are born into is not. We are born into an adult world that has followed tenets, structures, and traditions for generations. In meeting this adult world, we, as children, can be affected—positively and negatively—by the nature of that contact.

I used to believe that I was living authentically, true to my Self, but I wasn't. Even now, I sometimes ask myself, "Who is making this decision? Me? My ancestors? My parents? My culture? My teachers? My country?" How many threads of otherness do I still carry inside pulling my strings, directing my thoughts, manipulating my emotions, and controlling my behaviour?

The socialisation process, also referred to as "programming" or "conditioning," is usually gradual, subtle, and covert. No one tells us this is what has happened to us. The process is almost impossible to avoid and, once taken hold, difficult to shed. It is like a powerful virus that has infected the human population and is passed from one generation to the next by our families, our social institutions, our school system, our house of worship, and our nation. Almost everyone has the bug, but believes they are healthy.

We believe what the programming tells us about ourselves and about life, and live accordingly. The programme has an energy of its own and does not care about us. It suppresses the uniqueness of our individual soul, and stifles what our soul has incarnated to experience. It wants us to conform, to keep us impotent and fearful and easily controlled. The key to discovering the socialisation virus and knowing we are contaminated is through the process of awakening. Through self-enquiry, we open our eyes to this infection and the paths of transmission. Through dedication, we look for a cure. Through awakening, we end compliance and rediscover our originality.

Our Biological Body

The programming also affects our physical body. The biology of the body we inhabit has been on this planet for thousands of years, passed down from mother and father to daughter and son. The social conditioning of our ancestors is also ingrained in the physical body, resulting in attitudes and issues being transferred from one generation to the next. Consequently, not only do we carry the burdens of our current socialisation programming, but also we have an ancestral legacy of conditioning.

The Influence of Life Experiences

Life is unpredictable. In a moment our world can upend. One of my friends became a parent for the first time in 2010.

Four months later, the baby died. Upon becoming a parent, my friend felt immense joy, and then, only a short while later, he experienced the deep sorrow of Grace's passing. The experience changed his life perspective.

Small events can affect us, too. No matter how many controls we impose on ourselves and others to protect ourselves and try and prevent people and events from disrupting our life, things happen. If we do not deal with the little hurts and disappointments that these situations elicit, they too can stack up and create shadows and weight for us to carry.

When I was six years old, I forgot the lines of a poem during a school concert. My mind went blank even though I had practised the poem for weeks. It was one of those awful moments that seemed to last forever. As I went back to the classroom, still traumatised by what had happened, the teacher, whom I adored, brushed past me and said, "Useless child." For over forty years, I sought out the metaphorical background in life rather than the stage, and never learnt the words of another poem, even though I memorised countless essays to regurgitate in exams. In these ways, we silence ourselves, hinder our natural abilities and creative potential, and keep ourselves small.

Everything Counts

Irish visionary and social innovator Sister Stanislaus Kennedy writes, "There is no such thing as a meaningless moment or a meaningless life. If we are open to it, life will teach and shape us to become people of wisdom, compassion and joy, in our age, in our time."[2]

Everything that happens to us has the capacity to affect us—the smile of a stranger; an argument with the boss; the loss of a parent; bullying at school or the office; our first kiss; receiving a thank-you card; passing our driving test; making a mistake; being snubbed by a friend; laughing with a lover; dealing with illness; watching a movie; losing our phone; breaking up with our partner. Everything counts. Every experience has the potential to create an opportunity for growth.

Chapter 5

Separated from Our Divinity

A metaphor I have used for the human experience is a cake. The socialisation process is like the icing on top. The glaze has nothing to do with our authentic Self, but addicted to its sweetness and trapped by its gooeyness, we may be oblivious of the rest of the cake underneath.

The icing on the cake can vary in thickness. For some, the glaze is thin. For others, the glaze is heavy, holding in a great deal of trauma and hurt. The qualities of the barrier and our attitude towards the icing matter. For example, some people have overcome viscous icing by using adversity positively. Others, with only a slim coating, cling to it, fearful of what might happen if they let go.

The older we get, the harder and less malleable the icing can become. It can be easier to scrape it off when we are young. That said, it is never too late to start breaking up the glaze. The only things keeping the icing in place may be our dependency on it and emotional investment in it, our fear of change, and an unwillingness to challenge our thinking. Regardless of our age, when we stop feeding it and feeding off it, the glaze can crack open.

In July 2017, I sat in a café with my then-eighty-two-year-old Mum. She had always shied away from speaking about anything personal and had learnt to hide her emotions. As we sat sheltered from the rain, she started to cry. Mum said she was frightened by the deterioration of her body and mind. For half hour, as I held her hands, I spoke to Mum for the first time about her body, mind, stress, life, hurts, disappointments, and conditioning—all the things I have learnt in my personal journey. Mum listened, her tears subsided, we continued to hold hands, and at the end she said, "I have a lot to learn." Mum's icing cracked open that day.

Loss of Our Divine Connection

The most significant consequence of socialisation is the disconnection from our authentic Self, our heart, the Divine aspect within us, and the Divine outside of us, the Source that created all life. Is this why some of us are atheists? I know for myself that I had no interest in the Divine, God, or anything spiritual until my first awakening experience in 1995.

Indigenous shamans from many traditions advocate that the ennui and unhappiness, as well as many other mental and physical illnesses, are rooted in the soul level disconnection from Self and the Divine, which they see as the same. Instead of attempting to heal this inner separation, the conditioning encourages us to resolve our discontentment externally, through relationships with others, work, entertainment, and an endless collection of material goods. But nothing outside of us can ever fill the deep longing and emptiness caused by the severance from our authentic Self. Only through opening the doors of our mind and heart to the truth of who we are, can we hope to ease our malaise and restore our connection to joy.

The loss of Divine connection lowers our consciousness and inner resonance. Energy medicine teaches that everything has a vibration and that different mental and emotional states produce different vibrations within us.[1] As we are slowly engulfed in the planet's conditioning we start resonating with lower vibrational qualities such as fear and insecurity. We move away from the higher resonance of unconditional love we incarnate with. The conditioning then keeps us attached to this lower state of consciousness through its many manipulations, strategies, and distractions.

Birth of the Ego

The Earth's programming currently supports the development of the conditioned mind and ego. The more we immerse ourselves in the socialised reality around us, the more this reality influences us. We become what we see, hear, experience, and do. So from a pure state of being at birth, in childhood, we move into a state of conditioned thinking that, according to Aristotle, can govern the rest of our life.[2]

In psychology and philosophy, the ego has many different definitions. Ego is Latin for "I." For the purpose of this book, I view the ego as a by-product of the conditioned mind. It is the "I," the self we create as a result of our engagement with the socialisation process and life experiences.

An analogy is to an egg. Its shell is the ego that acts as

a buffer between us and the world. The egg white is the conditioned mind that surrounds the yolk, the wisdom mind of our authentic Self.

We can be so immersed in and attached to the social programming that we sincerely believe its stories. Life holds open new doors to wake us up from our misconceptions. Rather than walking through these new doors, most of the time we continue to walk through the old doors and on the familiar paths, even if they do not make us happy. In doing so, we maintain and reinforce our conditioned identity, our ego, and, in turn, the collective conditioning.

Believing is Seeing

For most of my life, I was a movie buff. After one film with a friend, we discussed a particular scene and interpreted it differently. My friend shook her head, "No, that's not what happened." I was sure I was right, as was my friend. Intrigued, we bought tickets to a later showing and watched the film again. At the end, we each saw the disputed scene exactly as before. I was confused.

I went to the film again, this time with the intention of seeing the truth of the scene no matter what it showed me. As the scene played out, I was stunned. It was exactly as my friend described it. This time, I saw it as she saw it. My judgement about the main character had skewed my initial interpretation of the events.

Our ego engages with life, which distorts our perception of what we see and filters what we take in.[3] Is this why our mind-sets may only allow us to see what we already believe? Good questions to ask yourself, "What do my beliefs tell me about myself and the world?" "Are these beliefs true?" "What are my beliefs preventing me from seeing?"

Ceremonies, spiritual practices that bring in the mystery of life, beyond the physical realm, can dislodge beliefs. For ten years, I took part in fire-dance ceremonies facilitated by the Native American shaman Emaho. In the fire-dance ceremony, Emaho puts his hand into a candle flame and then places it on a person's forehead as a healing blessing. Miraculously, his hand does not get burned. After one such ceremony, a longtime participant came up to Emaho. Astonished, he had only now seen Emaho put his hand into the flame without it burning. Even though the ceremony is the same each time, it took several years for the man to perceive that Emaho's hand went into the fire unscathed.

Automatic Pilot

It can be hard for us to know the extent to which our thinking and behaviour have been compromised by the conditioning. The threads of socialisation may be woven into every aspect of our life with such insidiousness and complexity that a great deal of our life can be stolen from us. When we live unconsciously, it is as if we are on automatic pilot, acting from habit rather than responsive choice. Habit limits our decision-making. We continually react to situations with the same coping strategies we learnt in childhood.

We drag around our past,
and let it shape our future.

Thus, the playground bully brings the same stance into adulthood, and becomes the office tyrant. The child who threw tantrums to get her needs met, turns into the manager who overreacts when the receptionist forgets to put milk in her coffee. The young girl who learnt to comply and obey in order to get the love and approval she yearned for, is the adult who cannot say no to anyone's demands. The teenage boy who is a perfectionist, grows into the supervisor who buries his head in the sand when things go awry.

Living on autopilot means we continue to act in the same way, day after day, month after month, year after year, without awareness of what we are doing. Then we may wonder why we keep meeting the same situations time and again. It is like getting on the same bus and being surprised when we keep arriving at the same destination. "Here again?!"

Summing-up

In incarnating on Earth we are born into a separate biological body, conditioned over generations; an established adult world of customs, languages, traditions, religious beliefs, rituals, social rules, laws, and attitudes; and a specific country within a particular era.

Not only does this programming diminish us, it can also affect our clarity. As children, we may have lacked the awareness and experience to know what was and was not helpful and appropriate to take on from the adult world. We simply absorbed much of what we were exposed to, as we were taught to do. By the age we could have made more perceptive choices, it was too late. Our identity and our worldview was already moulded by our social programming and life experiences.

Thus, from a state of pure consciousness at birth, we can end up enmeshed in a perspective shaped more by external influences, than reflective of our authentic Self. The extent to which each of us has disconnected from the truth of who we are and aligned with the social identity varies. Not everyone succumbs completely to the socialisation process. Some can retain a connection to their true Self and to the understanding that there is more to life than society's script.

But no matter our situation there is a way out. There is hope. We can learn. We can listen. We can turn our attention inwards, towards our authentic Self, our inner light, and nourish ourselves. In Part II we find out how to begin the process of self-discovery.

PART II

LEARNING NEW WAYS: THE MIND

Chapter 6

The Power of Awareness

We may or may not be able to change our outer circumstances, but with awareness we can always change our inner attitude, and this is enough to transform our life.[1] —Jack Kornfield, author and Buddhist practitioner

A Road Cannot Be Travelled without Taking a Step Forward

In 2003, I was on a five-day meditation retreat in St Andrews, Scotland, facilitated by the Zen Buddhist monk Thich Nhat Hanh. Each morning, Thay (teacher) gave a talk. At intervals, a monk or nun from the Community of Interbeing sounded a singing bowl. Everyone brought their attention inward and sat quietly for a few minutes. Then, Thay recommended the teaching. At the end of the first talk, I was struck by the harmonious interplay between Thay speaking and the ringing of the singing bowl. "How does the nun know when to sound the singing bowl?" I wondered.

The next day during Thay's talk, a monk sounded the singing bowl and we all took a sharp inhale. The sound of the bowl was disruptive. Thay turned to the monk and his irritation was clearly visible. The monk laughed nervously. Thay turned to the front and bent his head, connecting within. When he spoke again, he continued seamlessly with no residual irritation. I learnt a great deal from this experience.

Now, I understood how the monks and nuns knew when to ring the bell. When the monk sounded the bell, I, like Thay and many others, was jarred. The sound took us into the same disconnected space the monk was in.

*When we are connected with our Divine Self
we know what to do.*

Thay's reaction was also revelatory. In my naivety, I thought that advanced spiritual teachers had no reactions to everyday situations. Thay was clearly demonstrating this is not so. His reaction opened a door for me to relax with myself. In this conditioned world, no matter who we are, no matter how many years we do spiritual practice, we may still react to events. What is important is what we do with those reactions. Do we act out of them or do we, like Thay, detach from them, resume our inward connection, dissolve the reaction, and emerge in a state of harmony?

Know Yourself

Awareness is one of the four facets of awakening. Self-awareness helps us understand ourselves and learn from the situations and people we encounter. It derives from a process of self-enquiry that we can start to engage with at any time.

We do not need to wait for a crisis or a wake-up call to become self-aware.

We can develop awareness in five steps.

Step One: Become the Observer
An aspect of ourselves is capable of observing what we think, feel, and do as we go about our day. We can actively engage with our observer (aka witness or watcher) and consciously learn more about ourselves, cultivating self-awareness.

Pause here. Notice your thoughts. What are you thinking? Notice your feelings. How are you feeling? Notice your behaviour. How are you sitting? Where are your hands placed? You are now engaging your inner observer. According to Eckhart Tolle, engaging our awareness automatically disengages us from the external world and the lower vibration field of the conditioned mind. Being the observer connects us to a higher degree of consciousness.[2]

Awareness, also called mindfulness, will strengthen with practice, like a muscle. Throughout the day, make a conscious effort to observe yourself. For example, during the morning commute, walking to school to pick up the kids, even sitting on the toilet. It does not matter when we choose to watch ourselves, only that we do. We develop self-awareness and self-understanding through self-observation.

Step Two: Work the Small Stuff
If something happened to you during the day, for instance, you had an argument with your partner or got annoyed with the length of the supermarket queue, take time later to reflect on your thoughts and feelings during the situation and your subsequent actions. Some events can overwhelm us at the time and their impact becomes clear only afterwards. Other

situations, we may dismiss as insignificant, unaware that every event has the potential to show us something about ourselves, especially those that provoke emotional reactions. Ask, "What was I thinking and feeling as this happened?" This phrasing can make looking back more objective, less judgemental, and easier for your mind to accept. The aim is self-discovery, situation by situation.

When we dismiss minor incidents, life has a way of bringing us the same lesson again, sometimes with a harder nudge and bigger hurdle to attract our attention. Working the small stuff slowly and quietly, builds our confidence. By reflecting and making different choices in the way we think, feel, and act, we create changes in the way we live our life.

Step Three: Reflect and Release Stress

Our physical bodies hold the cellular memories of our experiences, particularly if an event impacted us strongly, and despite the passage of time.[3] Reflection can dislodge and release tension and stress, and avert a potential stress-induced illness or worsening health condition. Our systems have a limit to how much suppressed suffering they can endure before they start to break down.

As you reflect, notice gaps in your awareness. For instance, if you do not know how or what you felt in a situation, note that. Maybe you have never paid much attention to your feelings or your body. Allow yourself to access your feelings and any physical sensations without judgement.

Step Four: Learn for the Soul

When something happens to you, especially if it's upsetting, pull back from the situation and ask, "What is this situation teaching me about myself? What do I need to learn here?"

Look for the lessons in an event and ignore the drama. In this way, you mentally and emotionally disengage from the circumstances and any stories your mind wants to attach to what happened. View the event from the perspective of a lesson for your soul. Rereading your reflective journal (step five) after an incident and again a week later, may also bring insights.

Step Five: Write It Down
Journaling can help promote reflection and provide clarity and understanding. Writing encourages honesty and allows us to off-load our emotions about an event. In writing things down, concentrate on yourself, your thoughts, feelings, and actions, rather than on the other people in a situation, and do this without overfocussing on the story of what ensued. The story is rarely as important as your part in it. Like panning for gold, seek the nugget and allow the dross to fall away.

Awareness: It's Good for You

In his poem "To a Louse," the Scottish poet Robert Burns writes:

> "O wad some Powr the giftie gie us
> To see oursels as ithers see us!
> It wad frae monie a blunder free us,
> An' foolish notion:
> What airs in dress an' gait wad lea'e us,
> An' ev'n devotion!"[4]

Burns is asking for the gift of awareness, for he knows it would free us from many gaffes and reckless ideas. What else do you gain by becoming self-aware?

Benefit One: Be Here Now[5]

When we live without awareness, we can alternate between our memories of the past and projections of the future. The past and future are illusions. Our view of the past is subjective, influenced by our beliefs. And we project those same beliefs into the future and continue the misapprehension. Only the present exists. The beautiful thing about awareness is that it brings you into the present moment. The moment of possibility and potential.

Benefit Two: Create Space for a Different Outcome

Awareness allows you to pause between an event and your reaction to it. Pausing creates a gap that gives you the opportunity to decide how you are going to respond, and lets you see more clearly what is happening in a situation as it unfolds. Only then can you make more open-minded and empowered choices; say no, rather than the habitual yes, speak when you would normally stay quiet, or walk away when you would usually remain.

When a situation is unfolding, concentrate on not feeding the thoughts that arise or automatically following through with them. In that way, you prevent the thoughts from escalating and dictating your actions. In developing awareness, your responses are determined each time by a process of self-enquiry. Not everyone will respond to a situation in the same way, and no situation requires the same response. On another day, faced with a similar situation, you may respond differently. In each situation, aim to engage your awareness and then act objectively instead of being sucked into reactive, habitual behaviours.

Benefit Three: Make Better Choices

Every action has consequences. Whether the action is positive or negative, each has repercussions. The conditioned world operates under the spiritual law of cause and effect, sometimes referred to as the law of karma. Sometimes the consequences come quickly, which helps us see the karmic process in action. I give my friend a birthday present and she hugs me—action and consequence. Often the repercussions can take days, months, even years to manifest by which time, we may have forgotten the initial act. Regardless, when you act consciously, with awareness, you are more likely to accept the consequences and they are more likely to be favourable. Self-awareness fosters responsibility, maturity, and self-empowerment.

Benefit Four: Align with Your Soul's Plan

As you walk the path of awareness, you walk towards your authentic Self. Your authentic Self knows what you are here to do in this lifetime. It carries this wisdom. When you move in the direction of your true Self, you are automatically aligning yourself with your soul's path. You are on the way to fulfilling your soul's plan.

#

To develop awareness, we become the observer of our life events. We watch our thoughts and feelings committedly, without being ensnared. Through conscious thinking, we centre ourselves in the present and gather information from within and outside of ourselves. In the space of no action, we can choose objectively the most appropriate behaviour given the circumstance. Developing awareness is an essential ingredient for living in the moment and spiritual awakening. Awareness is a primary facet in opening the doors of our heart where ultimate freedom lies.

If we live our days the same—they stay the same.
If we want our future to be different,
we have to start responding differently
in the present moment.
To get different, we have to do different.
To do different, we have to know what we are
doing now.
To know what we are doing now, we engage
our awareness.
We become the observer.

Chapter 7

Applying Awareness

To introduce long-standing changes in our life that respect and support our authentic Self, we need self-awareness, followed by action based on this awareness; we see the unhealthy patterns and then uproot them. We can have awareness but unless we act accordingly, little will change in our life and we may become more unhappy. By applying our awareness, we flow with life towards joy.

See the Dream

Over the years, I have said countless times "I know, I know" about doing something beneficial. (And then, I did not do it.) What was stopping me turning my awareness into experience? By not applying my awareness, I remained trapped in my fear and dissatisfaction. That cycle eventually motivated me to act and hold the dream of what I wanted. Keep asking: Does this action take me closer to what I want? Does this thinking support my authentic Self?

Life Initiates Us

On the path of personal growth, we realise that life is our ally. Life brings us ideal situations and people to trigger our unhealthy behaviour and thought patterns. It also offers us personal challenges, such as a relationship breakdown, or health crisis. These are doors of initiation—opportunities for growth at soul level. We can use our self-awareness to see life's messages and choose appropriate ways to act. When we come through these initiations we are different, another part of the mask slips and we are birthed into a new perspective. Initiation is the second facet of awakening.

Even though our authentic Self knows a situation has the potential to heal the past and teach us something, our mind can become disheartened when faced with a challenge. So that we do not become overwhelmed, life helps us step-by-step and repetitively. Life will continue to bring us the next part of the jigsaw puzzle so that we can release the conditioning, and eventually complete the puzzle.

In 2005, I was about to deliver a training course for my employer. Two days prior to the course beginning, I met my manager in the office corridor. She informed me the project had been cancelled. I immediately felt an overwhelming sense of disappointment. When my manager said she had known for a week but had not told me, my anger surfaced and was directed at her. When I returned to my office, my colleagues witnessed my hurt as the tears flowed.

In a session that evening with my counselling supervisor, I was able to separate my emotional reaction of anger and hurt, from the situation: the project cancellation. I saw how inappropriate my misplaced anger onto my boss was. I apologised to my manager the next day.

Three months later, another piece of the jigsaw appeared. I experienced another unexpected loss—my flat, which produced the same response in me. Different situation, same reaction. This time, as the feelings of anger and sadness arose, I walked to a local park and gave myself the space to experience the whole mental and emotional roller-coaster. When the anger surfaced, I did not direct it at anyone; instead I breathed deeply, shook it out of me, and offered it to the Earth to transform. (I use a spiritual practice, in which I symbolically bury the anger in the Earth. The Earth has the power to transform negative energy into positive light.) When the pain came, I let the tears flow without fuelling the hurt with poor me stories.

I observed myself through the entire process, the sinking feelings of pain intertwined with fear and a victim's attitude of unfairness. As the pain took me into tears, the anger arose and rescued me from vulnerability and gave me a sense of power. Eventually, as I released the pain through the tears, the thoughts and feelings quietened. Later, I reflected to better understand my reactions and gain more objectivity.

The following month brought the next jigsaw piece. After waiting four months for an assistant in a new work project, I was informed that Eric, whom I had trained for three weeks, was moving to a different project. Instantly, the familiar reactions around loss were triggered. This time instead of focussing on the hurt, I concentrated on the facts of the situation. Eric was joining a project better suited to his skills. As I breathed and acknowledged this, the hurt eased. With awareness and space, I was able to experience, manage, and process my reaction internally, and still converse with Eric's supervisor who delivered the news. When I met Eric after the meeting, I sat down and wrote him a good reference.

These three experiences around the issue of loss taught me:

- My attitude was responsible for my pain, not the situations or the people involved.
- I can process the feelings and thoughts coming up and choose another way of responding.
- I can develop a healthier, less fearful relationship with my vulnerability.
- Life brought me these situations (aka initiation) to help me address this issue.
- I am stronger than the conditioned mental and emotional reactions and stronger than I thought.
- Each successive situation becomes easier to deal with.

Remaining open and present to experience what each moment is offering brings you a more flexible and expansive path, a return of your authentic power, and more lasting happiness.

Learn Your Triggers

As the story above illustrates, it is crucial to learn what triggers a reaction in you, positive and negative. What happened most recently? How did it end? Triggers are a signal to pause, engage self-awareness, and observe. Ask: What emotions and mind-sets are rising within me that need my attention? What behaviour would my usual reaction elicit?

Despite what our mind would have us believe, our reactions to people and events are our responsibility. No matter what we might think, or how we might try to justify our emotional outbursts and blame another person, we are responsible for our feelings and actions. When we hold a grudge against someone or a situation, we are the one left carrying the weight.

Acknowledging and taking responsibility for your emotional reactions is a crucial aspect of personal development and social intelligence. It is up to you to become aware of your triggers and work out how to respond appropriately. Remember, life will help you.

Build New Neural Pathways

Scientific research in the field of neuroplasticity shows that with awareness it is possible to rewire our brain and achieve different outcomes.[1] Our physiology will support us to break free from unhealthy habits.

For example, I decided to watch myself buying CDs (compact music disks), which had become a three-CD splurge every Friday lunchtime. In the first weeks, I found myself back at work with three new CDs and no memory of what had happened. Then one day, I saw myself standing at the shop counter holding three CDs. In that moment, I had a choice: buy the CDs or put them back. I put them back. Alas, my habit was not broken. Another day, I observed myself in the shop flipping through CD cases. I walked out of the shop. It was another stage in the process. Over the next few weeks, I watched myself standing outside a music shop and choosing not to go in, or walking past the shop. Then, a light bulb moment, I decided to read a book in the park during Friday lunch.

It took me four months to build a new neural pathway and break the habit. The experience showed me how blind I was about my behaviour, how strong habits can be, and that although breaking them is not always straightforward, it is biologically feasible. I also had to release any self-judgement at not being able to change immediately. It took time, perseverance, and effort.

By overcoming your habitual patterns, you are uncovering your true Self. It is always there.

Point of Freedom

Years ago, in New Zealand, I attended a talk by a Buddhist teacher about the space that we create between our arising feelings and thoughts and any subsequent action. He called this space the "point of freedom." At that point, with awareness, we have the opportunity to change our behaviour. The freedom the Buddhist teacher referred to, is the freedom from the unhealthy habit pattern.

When we miss this point, we will be caught up in the usual cycle of suffering and pain our reactive actions cause. To ensure that you do not miss this point, you can coax yourself towards a new perspective in many ways. You can set an intention to be free of the habit. As the habit unfolds you can pause. You can walk away. You can disengage from the voice of the mind. You can focus on your breath instead of the reactive thoughts and feelings. You can choose a different response.

If you miss the freedom moment and react, use self-forgiveness and compassion. Say, "It's OK. Next time, I can respond better." It takes practice to alter our ingrained ways. Again,

life will continue to bring us situations to help us change...
until we do. This is life's way of supporting us to wake up.

#

How can we be involved, be part of the world, but not
caught by it? This is the secret, finding the eternal balance.
This is why awakened teachers advocate self-awareness and
personal development as a way of transforming ourselves
and the collective conditioning. As we shake off the lower
vibrations of the programming, our individual consciousness
is raised, and our higher awareness and positivity has a
beneficial effect on others.

Chapter 8

Respecting the Mind

In 2009, in the first weeks after awakening from the coma in Peru and experiencing life without thoughts, I know I am not the conditioned ego mind. My limited view was expanded to encompass the enlightened state. In that state, I understood a truth in Shakespeare's *Hamlet*, "[F]or there is nothing either good or bad, but thinking makes it so."[1] Six months after the coma, fully integrated in my body, I also observed how I could still be influenced by the conditioned mind and its ego structure, although not to the same degree as before. Now I wanted to discover how to break free of the mind's control and limitations and return to the awakened, thought-free state.

The Different Aspects of the Mind

In many philosophical and psychological disciplines, various words have been used to describe different aspects of the mind. I am clarifying the terms in the context of this book.

Wise teachers speak of the enlightened mind as the "big" mind, the wisdom mind of our essential nature. (Wise teachers is my term for the enlightened spirit beings who support me personally and professionally. These wise beings are universal and offer their insights throughout the book.)

In contrast, the conditioned mind has been referred to as the "small" mind, or the "everyday" mind. Jung proposed that within the conditioned mind, the conscious part is what we are aware of, and the unconscious or "shadow" part is what we are not aware of.[2] In this book, I use "the mind" for the conditioned aspect and otherwise, "the wisdom mind." In chapter 14, I talk about the shadow.

Further, the wise teachers say that here on Earth humans associate the mind with the brain, but they are not the same. The enlightened mind and the unenlightened, conditioned mind are aspects of the heart, and they affect and govern the brain as well as the rest of the body. The enlightened mind is the wise part of the heart. The unenlightened mind is the hurt part. In the heart, the unenlightened mind lies in front of the enlightened mind like a veil. Through our spiritual practices and personal work, we lift the veil and open the door to the enlightened mind, the enlightened state.

In a meditation, I was shown that the mind is the intelligence that governs the body and brain. When we are in our enlightened mind, our body and brain are in harmony. When we are in our ego mind, the body and brain are compromised by our conditioned mind-sets, and can become unbalanced and potentially dis-eased.

The Importance of the Mind

We need our mind. We could not function with the practical aspects of life without it. The mind develops a frame of reference about our world, so that we can make sense of and negotiate our everyday life. The mind also holds information that we can use to develop strategies and better navigate situations. When we engage with our mind in a constructive way, we can look to the past and see what has worked for us and apply that knowledge to our present circumstances. Later, we can reflect on what happened and, if necessary, update what we learnt from the new situation.

The mind is also an essential aspect of us; we are born with the wisdom mind. Then through the socialisation process, we adapt and develop the ego mind. Our spiritual practices and personal work help us slowly transmute the egoic part of the mind. We awaken into the wisdom mind. We come full circle; from no ego, to ego, to no ego.

Features of the Mind

Our mind is not fixed. It can change. We can harness the mind's ability to transform and direct it towards supporting our authentic Self.

Malleable. We can open our mind to new perspectives, which can guide us to more helpful viewpoints and outcomes. As well as watching and learning from ourselves, we can acquire understanding through witnessing others and the natural world. Through reflection and inquiry, our mind can be retrained.

For instance, when our version of reality does not agree with someone else's, the mind may feel threatened. We can become confused, indignant, angry, and upset, and allow ourselves to be drawn into drama. Equally, when we tell our story, we can exaggerate our pains and the injustices and omit information that does not support our cause, to garner sympathy. Misery loves company. We can reeducate the mind to stop responding to others' (and our own) need for validation.

Thinking critically, exercising discernment. Our adult mind has the capacity to think critically and develop discernment. As we open to different outlooks, we can choose what to take on, keep, or put aside. We can observe people, and let their actions speak as opposed to their words or our expectations and assumptions. Rather than automatically accepting someone because they are famous, wear a robe, talk a good talk, make promises, or are in a position of authority, we can be judicious about whom we listen to, associate with, and believe.

The mind is a powerful tool when it believes something. Witness the power of the placebo effect.

Concentration and focus. We can learn to use the power of the mind to focus and concentrate on specific tasks or even states of being. (We will explore meditation as a self-awareness tool in chapter 17.) Focussing on what supports our inner growth can help us align our mind and our thinking to that perspective.

You could adopt the strategy of asking your mind to support your awakening. For instance, whenever I experience a positive state such as happiness, I say to my mind, "This is what I want more of. Help me become happier." And it has.

Open-minded. Our beliefs create expectations that inevitably lead to disappointment. Become aware when your mind assumes something and pull back. Adopt a more open-minded attitude. You can say to your mind, "I see what you expect. Let's wait and see what happens."

Positive thinking. We can train our mind to be more affirmative, to orientate to the positive. Positive psychology research shows that factors such as optimism, trust, forgiveness, spirituality, honesty, perseverance, and the ability to be in flow with life can offset mental illness in people.[3]

Relaxation. We can access and use our imagination to bring different pictures into our mind, which can take us from a state of anxiety and tension to one of growing relaxation and calm.[4] Anxiety often escalates because we are choosing, albeit unconsciously, to fixate on what is worrying us. Energy flows to whatever we focus our attention on. If we think of something calming and uplifting, our energy will move in that direction.

Become aware when you are caught in apprehension, and then consciously redirect your awareness with the intention of relaxing. Try meditation, listen to calming music, go for a walk in nature, think a positive thought, recall something funny and laugh, or take slow deep breaths.

Discover which relaxation techniques work best for you and utilise them, especially if your mind is programmed to worry. There is a saying in my country that someone can "worry for Scotland." It is used to describe anyone who frets a lot. I inherited this anxiety from my mum, as she did from her mum, and probably for many generations back. By the time I was a teenager, I lived in a constant state of alertness and catastrophic thinking. In my mid-twenties, when I emigrated to New Zealand, I discovered a much more open and relaxing environment and culture. The local attitude of "she'll be right," all will be well, sums up their positivity. Exposure to this new outlook was incredibly freeing for my body, mind, and spirit.

Insights. The mind's ability to relax and soften opens up the potential for insights to arise from within. There is a possibility of gaining more understanding and wisdom from difficult situations, even pinpointing the underlying cause. In the exercise below, you can practice relaxing your ego mind and becoming aware of information held within your wisdom mind.

#

As we gradually retrain the mind to use its skills constructively, align our thinking with our authentic Self, and move away from the programming that manifests repetition and regurgitation, we strengthen the connection to our enlightened mind. This allows us access to our inherent creativity and clear thinking as we step more fully into our authentic power.

Some years ago, I chose to stop watching television, even though it had been a way of switching off from pressures at work. When I watched TV, especially the news, I was opening a door to an influx of negativity and drama that was reinforcing old patterns of thinking.

As well as an increasing body of psychological research, there are many anecdotal stories of people improving their physical health by engaging their mind in a positive way. For example, when Norman Cousins, an American political journalist, was diagnosed with a crippling and irreversible disease and given a 1 in 500 chance of recovery, he actively sought alternate ways to regain his health rather than remain a passive observer. Ten minutes of belly laughter gave him two hours of pain free sleep, when nothing else, not even morphine, helped. Cousins eventually regained the full function of his body.[5]

Exercise 1. Relaxing the Mind with a Four-Count Breath

To help you relax and gain understanding by refocusing your attention.

1. Sit quietly for a few minutes. Notice how you are feeling. Consciously intend to quieten your mind.

2. Bring your awareness to your breath. Breathe in for a count of four, hold your breath for a count of four, breathe out for a count of four, hold your breath out for a count of four. Repeat the sequence three more times. Then, allow your breathing to return to normal.

3. As you inhale, imagine breathing in space. As you exhale, imagine all the tension leaving your body and the space remaining. Continue for a few minutes, and let the feeling of expansion and relaxation grow and deepen. (If your attention wanders at any time, gently disengage from the thoughts and bring your focus back to your breath, without judgement.)

4. Visualise a place where you feel safe and at ease. It could be a room in your home, a place in nature, or somewhere else real or imagined. Picture this place now. Look around you, what do you see? Is the temperature cool or warm? Is there a breeze, or is the air still? How do you feel? What can you smell and touch? Stay in this space for ten minutes, intending that every cell of your body is bathed in the peace you feel.

5.   While in your safe space, reflect on what lies beneath the anxiety. Ask, "What is this anxiety about?" Wait to see if any images, thoughts, or feelings arise. Do not judge or dismiss anything. Ask, "Is this worry genuine?" Again, wait to see what answer comes to you. Ask, "What can I do to ease my anxiety?"

6.   Gently bring yourself back by becoming conscious of your surroundings and opening your eyes. Thank yourself for taking the time to relax. Notice how you feel. Are there any positive differences? The mind needs evidence to accept change, so consciously acknowledge how this exercise helps you.

By focusing on your breath, you automatically bring yourself into the here and now of the present moment. You can use this strategy at any time. Taking a conscious deep breath in and out is one of the fail safe ways to interrupt the conditioned mind's stream of thoughts.

The hardest time to make the effort to relax is often the time we need it most. When we are anxious and stressed, the mind will often find countless excuses to stop us from sitting down and relaxing, even for a few minutes. Yet, we have the capacity to redirect our mind to positive thoughts and transform our inner landscape to tranquility.

Chapter 9

Taking Back Our Power

In this chapter, we learn the ways our mind tries to limit us and how we can take back our power.

Countering the Mind's Strategies

The ego mind is insecure and will develop strategies to protect itself and stay in command. When the mind tries to control us, we have many resources and techniques to stay on top.

Banal, blameshifts, and judgement. Our mind chatter can feel greedy and voracious—seemingly incessant, sometimes inane, sometimes disturbing, and often distracting. Our mind has learnt to complain and blame others and the situation for our unhappiness and suffering. Bemoaning strengthens the victim mentality and reinforces our attachment to helplessness. We keep our vibration low as we envelop ourselves in a cloud of outrage and feelings of powerlessness. We become vulnerable to thoughts that are untrue (false pretence and denial); imaginary about the future (what-if thinking); and irrelevant to the current situation (distractions). Judgemental thoughts and other defences undermine our Self and others and waste vital time and energy. The key is to notice them, regulate your response and take back your sovereignty.

Power grabs. To protect ourselves from hurt and disappointment, the ego seeks power and control. Not content with controlling just ourselves, the mind may seek to impose its will on others. Our self-awareness can help us understand the suffering we cause ourselves and others with our skewed ideas about power. In reality, the only thing we are in charge of is our responses, and only when we are self-aware.

Energy drains. Lethargy, numbing out, and procrastination can cripple our mind from acting in our best interest. Lethargy opts for comfort and familiarity over change. Numbing out with substance abuse or repetitive passivity dulls our senses. Vacillation thwarts our acting upon opportunities. Sometimes the mind's chatter can be tenuous. When we challenge it and choose to support our authentic Self over the ego's ramblings, the chatter often dissolves.

Rushed and rash. We are accustomed to instant results. Flick a switch and the light comes on. When we flick the switch of inner awakening and the light is slow to ignite, we can be quick to give up. Our expectations may be too high and our patience, too low. Racing through life robs us of the experience of being fully present and alive in the now.

With presence, we can make the decisions that support the authentic Self. Waiting to decide is a valid option, too. We do not need to answer every question we are asked instantly or at all. We can allow ourselves to be in a place of not knowing that permits things to unfold organically and creatively.

In 2008 when I returned to Scotland from overseas travels, I had no idea where I would find work. I only knew that I wanted to live in Glasgow and work in the therapeutic field. A few days later, a friend called to tell me about a part-time counselling and therapist post. I applied, and three weeks later was offered the job. This is the magic we can open ourselves up to.

The joy of wrong. Even without its accelerated pace, the mind can stoke our anxieties—especially our fear of failure. The mind is a charmer. It wants to look good, sound clever, and be right. It seeks out evidence to confirm existing beliefs (known as "confirmation bias") and rationalises the rest. It feels threatened if challenged. Owning our mistakes and lack of knowledge in front of others can be embarrassing, but is ultimately empowering and an opportunity to learn, grow, and move away from fear.

An Eastern Framework—The Five Poisons

Tibetan Bön Buddhism speaks about the five poisons that create pain and suffering in every aspect of our being and keep us separated from our natural state—that of unconditional love. The five poisons (known as kleshas, in Sanskrit) are: attachment, jealousy, anger, pride, and ignorance. We can be enveloped in the negativity of the poisons for days to even a lifetime, spew out toxic energy, and create more karma for ourselves and a karmic link to others. In the bigger picture, where all life is interconnected, we also poison the environment with our negativity.

I have had an indelible experience with one of these poisons: pride. Staying for a month in the home of one of my teachers, Emaho, I was offered the large guest room, with a double bed, walk-in wardrobe, en suite facilities, and balcony. It was the most beautiful of rooms, and I was in heaven. One morning towards the end of my stay, Emaho asked me to move out of the room as a couple were coming to stay for a few days. I cleaned the room and moved into a shared bedroom. Then, I went for a lovely walk in town.

When I returned, Emaho called everyone into the en suite bathroom of the large guest room. He spoke at length about what it means to be a good guest in someone's house. He showed us all the places that had not been cleaned properly, including marks on the walls, hairs behind the bathroom door, dust on the headboard. I was mortified.

As Emaho spoke, I consciously engaged my wise Self and focussed on what he said rather than be pulled into the mental and emotional dramas unleashing within. Instinctively, I knew he was giving me an important lesson. As I listened, flashbacks surfaced showing me the times Emaho had witnessed my pride.

Immediately after Emaho spoke, everyone started to clean the house. Two hours later, my mind and emotions were finally at peace and I was physically exhausted. I went to Emaho's room and thanked him for the lesson. He smiled and said, "You're welcome." I smiled back and left. It was a painful teaching, but one I have never forgotten.

I have shared this story with friends, all of whom found it harsh. Going through the experience was certainly difficult; yet, I never regarded it as harsh. My ego was shaken, not my authentic Self. Reflection has shown me Emaho's compassion towards my true Self. Not once did he personalise what he said. He made his point without accusation or judgement. He gave me the opportunity to realign with my true Self, and I took it.

Sandra Ingerman, an American writer, teacher, and visionary, said, "It is who we become that changes the world not what we do."[1] When we overcome life's initiations, we empower ourselves from within and walk away renewed. This brings positive change to ourselves and the world.

Five Approaches to Change Our Relationship to the Mind

Our ego mind creates stories, but we are not helpless. By mastering the mind's root causes of suffering, we can develop a different relationship to the mind. We can learn to respect it without ceding power to it.

Be selective. Be discerning about what you take on from others. Think more critically. Be a healthy skeptic. Don't believe everything you think or hear. Guide the mind towards what serves your authentic Self. Ask, "Does this thought (or behaviour) take me towards my true Self, or away?" Be honest with yourself and others. Stop rationalising, justifying, and lying.

Practise healthy detachment. Stay in the space of the observer. Detaching is not about disengaging emotionally, numbing out, or giving up. Detachment is a gradual energetic withdrawal of your focus and power from the external world, and a refocusing of your energy within. In detaching, you stop supporting what does not belong to you and nourish what does, your essential Self. As T. S. Eliot says, "In order to possess what you do not possess you must go by the way of dispossession."[2]

Work with anger and pride. Become OK with mistakes; they are part of learning. Relax and quiet your mind through conscious breathing. Look for the good, including acts of kindness.

Live and learn. Dispel ignorance with wisdom.

Make the conditioning your ally. By separating you from your Divine nature, the conditioning gives you the opportunity to rediscover your authentic Self.

Sometimes it is only through the experience of what you are not that you can truly appreciate what you are.

It takes time to understand how the conditioning misleads us, and change our relationship towards it. The conditioning is a powerful force that is sneaky and stubborn. It wants its cake, but you can say, "I'm not going to feed you."

The Same Old Feelings

We can identify three distinct feeling tones of the mind (attachment, aversion, and neutrality), but how do we respond when one mind state predominates? For example, as a child, I experienced numerous instances of being ridiculed. For years when I was put on the spot or became the focus of attention, I developed an aversion to this state and became immobilised with fear. The pattern was predictable.

We all attract scenarios that elicit our habitual response. Why? Because these events and the people involved expose deeper, hidden pain that we need to heal in order to evolve into the authentic Self. As we realise this bigger picture and face these life tests with honesty, integrity, and openheartedness, we grow and mature. Conversely, when we run from these challenges using strategies of avoidance and distraction, we perpetuate a state of inner suffering and the cycle of trials.

Each trial presents a choice. Either be ensnared by the latest drama and your part in it and acquiesce, or flaunt the rules and break free. How? Break attachment with detachment. Face what is underneath aversion. Find the neutral space of the observer.

Games People Play[3]

The most common game we play out is a duel between a winner and a loser. The victim is hurt by the perpetrator. The bumbler is set right by the fixer. The damsel-in-distress is rescued by the knight in shining armour. Wise teachers say that our soul makes agreements with other souls prior to incarnation to experience these games, to learn from both happiness and suffering, in order to evolve personally and spiritually.

When I work with clients, we usually identify one or two main themes running through all their stories. Outside of the therapeutic context, we can notice if there are any patterns or issues that keep repeating. For instance, do we fall in love with the same personality type? Do we end up in jobs with managers who disregard us? Do we allow friends and family members to walk over us? Until we resolve the main scripts, we will continue to be called back for reruns—attracting particular situations and people to help us become aware of the pattern and eventually heal.

Stop Playing the Game

When you identify a pattern, even when you do not understand its larger issues, acknowledge it. Ask, "What am I doing to keep up (or stay in) the game?" Then stop. Let it go. Resent picking up your partner's dirty socks? Don't pick up your partner's dirty socks. When we remove ourselves from the games we play with others, there is a good chance that the game will end, perhaps not right away, but in time. Meanwhile, we feel liberated and uplifted, grow in self-esteem, and release an emotionally toxic pattern.

Visualisation is a powerful tool to rewrite the script. For example, with a young client Graeme who endured playground bullying, I asked him to imagine himself pulling back his energy from the other boy. Then Graeme envisioned himself as strong and confident, seeing himself standing in his own power and the other boy ignoring him. Graeme established clear personal boundaries. He practiced the visualisation twice daily (before school and before bedtime).

In addition, since the other boy must have had something upsetting going on in his life, I asked Graeme to go into his heart and after his visualisation, send good thoughts to the other boy.

Lastly, Graeme and I did a ceremony from Toltec Shamanism to cut the energetic connections between him and the other boy. Ceremonies can be powerful tools for initiating change in our life especially when done wholeheartedly with a pure intention. The day after we did the ceremony, the bullying stopped.

Changing our habitual responses to our life's scripts is uncomfortable, but necessary so we can heal. Supporting our authentic Self sometimes requires writing new tenets.

PART III

LISTENING TO INNER WISDOM: THE BODY

Chapter 10

Facing Our Emotions

Emotions are part of the gift of experiencing life in a physical body. A healthy flow of feelings can support us through life's upheavals and open us to a bigger awareness. For instance, the grieving process moves us from feelings of loss to a place of acceptance. Frustration nudges us from procrastination into action. Love opens the door to the richness and beauty of life. Anger can be the catalyst for change. Yet, for some of us, experiencing our feelings is difficult. In this chapter, we learn how to appreciate and work with our emotions in a healthy way.

Emotions—Learned Responses to What Happens to Us

Emotions are the labels we give to various energetic responses to our and other's actions and the situations we encounter. We learn emotions, such as sadness, fear, anger, disappointment, and shame, through the socialisation process. We were not born with these different emotions—only the felt senses of unconditional love and the qualities of the enlightened state.

Having learned human emotions, we then identify with them and adopt beliefs that reinforce them. We speak of ourselves as if we are our emotions. "I am sad." "I am embarrassed." But an emotion is not a fait accompli (when A happens, I must feel B). Rather, we have many options to appropriately and responsibly manage our emotions.

From Emotional Suppression to Healthy Engagement

Sensations arise in the body before we attach meaning to them. We associate a lump in the throat with anxiety and grief, and butterflies in our stomach and sweaty palms with nervousness. The physical manifestation is objective. The meaning we attach to it is not. It is coloured by the conditioning. The first step out of the chicken-or-the-egg conundrum is to maintain awareness of the physical sense and not identify with its purported meaning and our beliefs.

We are looking behind the emotional curtain—quite the opposite of the more common strategies to keep our feelings at bay. Keep conversations superficial. Live in the mind. Numb out. Stay busy. Fill the silence. Shield with anger. Drown our sorrows in drink. Meanwhile, an emotional time bomb ticks away inside. From an early age, I learned to suppress my feelings and my internal, rage-filled volcano would erupt every six months or so. I finally broke the pattern in my forties when I allowed myself to start feeling some of the pain that the anger masked.

According to Scotland-based homeopath John Carlin, the negative energy of stored emotions is like a pollution that is "non-self-limiting;"[1] it grows in force over time. Without intervention, such as with homeopathy, complementary therapy, counselling, and personal work, trapped emotions can eventually lead to debilitating, chronic, and life-threatening illnesses.

Being hurt in itself may be life's way of trying to open our heart and wake us up from the conditioning. Appreciating life's lessons, even the hard ones, can lead to positive change and inner transformation, as my experience below demonstrates.

Two years after his cancer diagnosis, my Dad, now deceased, was still in shock. Paradoxically, the cancer which was threatening to take Dad from us, brought our family closer together. Dad's cancer was an opportunity for each of us to examine our relationship with Dad and with each other, and even with ourselves. One night, Dad and I talked about his condition and his attitude to it. Afterwards, he said, "I wish we had spoken like this years ago." I said, "I wish we had, too, Dad."

But, the beautiful thing is, we had the opportunity. The cancer gave Dad and I the gift of candor, and facilitated my own emotional review. This experience opened me further to the fragility of life on Earth. Unlike in the past, I now cry easily from memories of joy and past hurts. Each is a blessing—of gratitude and love for my life and for all that I have experienced. I know these tears of love and pain are the tears of grace. My tender, strong human heart, holding pain and joy, is bursting with emotion and my job is to allow its expression.

Your Emotions and Your Responsibility

In her TED Talk, English author and my friend Madeleine Black says, "It's not what happens to us in life that is important, but what we do with it that really matters."[2] These are profound words. If we were to fully appreciate their significance and live accordingly, we could transform our lives. Although we cannot change an event, we can free ourselves from its hold over us. In the following section, I show how we can extend our awareness to our feelings and release the trapped dissatisfaction and hurt. This purification process is the third facet of awakening.

The degree to which we accept self-responsibility for our own healing is the extent to which we can allow whatever happens to us to become an opportunity for personal growth and emotional maturity. Without self-blame or judgement, we become more honest with ourselves, and allow in more awareness and objectivity. We slowly release our hurts and stand taller in our life.

Emotional Release Breathing: Setting Yourself Free

The first step is to acknowledge our emotions and then work to release the energy of the hurts, disappointments, and traumas that is held in the physical body's tissues. We can do this through various techniques: movement, such as shaking or dancing; spiritual practices, such as yoga and meditation; bodywork, such as therapeutic massage and sacral cranial therapy; and alternative therapies, like EMDR (Eye Movement Desensitisation and Reprocessing) and breath work.

One of the most powerful and transforming experiences I have had was taking part in breath work seminars. Participants are encouraged to breathe deeply into their body, until they automatically start to release the negative emotional energy from past events that is held internally. As stated by Dr Judith Kravitz, an international expert in integrative breath therapy, focussed, conscious breathing "activates a high frequency of electromagnetic vibration throughout the body and mind. According to the scientific principle of Entrainment, low frequency energy patterns are raised and transformed in the presence of the higher frequency energy state. This clears blockages within the energy systems."[3]

From my breath work experience, counselling courses, personal development workshops, and energy healing seminars, I found a way to experience my feelings that I have continued practicing for many years. I teach the method that I call emotional release breathing (ERB) to my clients, many of whom, like me, were emotionally withdrawn. I include the method here to support, guide, and show you what to do.

Exercise 2. Emotional Release Breathing (ERB)

To help you experience and release feelings in a healthy way.

1. When you sense a feeling in the body, make a conscious decision to experience it. Say, "Welcome." (If you can't do it in the moment then return to the feeling later.)

2. Sit down, and keep the spine erect. Engage the observer.

3. Breathe deeply—as if inhaling space into the body and power into the spine.

4. Breathe into the area where the feeling is and connect with the energy of the feeling. Allow the energy of the feeling to begin to move.

5. Keep breathing and tracking the feeling as the energy moves. You may shake, swallow, move your jaw, yawn or burp, lift your shoulders, and turn your neck and head to help the body relax and release the energy and any associated tension.

6. Don't stoke the feelings with thoughts. Detach from your mind and experience the sensations.

7. Ride the feeling waves, and keep breathing deeply. Stay with the process until the waves subside and your body is calm.

8. Gently bring your focus back out into the room. Notice how your mind and body feel now.

The length of each ERB process will vary depending on the strength of the triggered feelings and your familiarity with the method. Also, some emotional hurts are deep and you may revisit them again and again until they are finally resolved. Others will move through your body more easily.

According to Jill Bolte Taylor, an American neuroanatomist and author, a triggered emotional reaction produces a release of chemicals from our limbic system in the brain. She states, "Once triggered, the chemical released by my brain surges through my body and I have a physiological experience. Within ninety seconds from the initial trigger, the chemical component of my anger has completely dissipated from my blood and my automatic response is over."[4] Thus, if a wave lasts longer than ninety seconds, thoughts may be fuelling the feelings.

You may feel sore, tingly, or nauseous during and after the practice. This is common and due to stagnant emotional energy releasing from the body. You may also feel lighter, more spacious. Be gentle with yourself. Drinking water afterwards continues the purification process. This is physical work and the body needs time to recover.

Physical and emotional pain cause us to automatically tense up and stop breathing, retaining the hurt. This exercise is effective because it does the opposite: relax and breathe.

A complementary technique that I also use combines the ERB with focussing as described by American author and educator, Ann Weiser Cornell, PhD, in her book *The Power of Focusing.*[5] This is helpful if the feeling (energy) does not move as you breathe into it.

Acknowledge any discomfort around the energy block, and thank it for drawing your attention to it. Get a sense of the block. What is its shape, colour, texture? Once you acknowledge it, does it remain static, or move to another area of the body and change in some way? Ask of the block, "Do you have anything to tell me? Is there something you would like me to be aware of?" By studying aspects of the block instead of perceiving only its discomfort, you may gain new insights.

Behind the Stories: Finding the Diamond underneath the Pain

In the ERB practice, it is important to be with your raw feelings without adding thoughts from the mind. Maintain focus in the body and feel the sensations until they cease. The aim is to experience and stay with the energy of the emotion as it moves through and out of the body. Using this approach, I have experienced emotions of shame, anger, hurt, fear, sadness, disappointment, pain, joy, happiness, and frustration, as well as resistance. This practice has empowered me.

Then, one day as I was working with the practice, letting the feelings arise and shift, I discovered something. There is a still space beyond all the feelings and resistance, a place of nothingness that is absolutely alive. This is the void, the emptiness of our infinite being. Beyond all the thoughts and feelings we uncover the diamond, the pure consciousness of our authentic Self. "The diamond discovered *is you*." says Gangaji.[6]

Commit to the Process

The intention of all spiritual practice and personal development is to meet the Self firsthand, unmediated by the ego, our emotions, and our story. The doorway to the authentic Self is through the physical and emotional body while detaching from the human conditioning. We adopt the witness consciousness. This is not as easy as it may sound. We are frightened and insecure. Who would we be without our pain, our stories, our reference points, our framework?

The American writer James Baldwin said, "Not everything that is faced can be changed. But nothing can be changed until it is faced."[7] Here are three suggestions to help you do just that, or in the words of a popular phrase: to face it till you erase it.

Persevere. When you meet fear head-on, you often learn that the bark is worse than the bite. Persist through the different layers of resistance. Stay with the emotional wave right to the end and experience the peace beyond the conditioned feelings.

Learn. This practice shows you there is a healthy and safe way to engage with your feelings and learn about yourself.

Grow in intimacy and kindness. You may find that your relationship with yourself and your body changes through this process—becoming softer, gentler, kinder, and less judgemental. Judgement in any form stops the flow of awakening.

When you face your feelings, you discover allowance and self-acceptance. Through a combination of conscious feeling, breathing, focussing, and relaxing, you learn that you can be with emotional pain and disappointment, and move from a place of emotional drama or avoidance to a place of emotional freedom and maturity. You allow yourself to walk the path of transformation: letting the butterfly slowly emerge from its cocoon.

All Will Pass

In the natural order of things, everything passes, our sadness, joy, frustration, happiness, anger, peacefulness, all pass in time. Things come and go—despite how we may cling to them. For instance, if we are sad and the feeling and story of our sadness is what we dwell on, we magnify the sadness. Our focus and incessant thoughts give the sadness more energy and this creates more unhappiness. Alternatively, if we allow ourselves to experience the sadness without attaching thoughts to it, the feeling will pass. When we are aware of our feelings in this organic way, we see the transient nature of our body and of life. We have evidence of the illusionary nature of the conditioning, what Buddhism refers to as the impermanence of all things.

Chapter 11

Working with Anger and Fear

[W]e have wasted too much, much too much strength and time on getting angry and getting even with others in a helpless shadow theatre which only we, who suffered impotently, knew anything about.[1] —Pascal Mercier, pseudonym of Peter Bieri, Swiss writer and philosopher.

I get up early to meditate so that I can leave Mum's house at 7:30 a.m. and drive back to my flat in Glasgow for my monthly healing exchange with my friend Yvonne. While making breakfast, I check my phone and see Yvonne's text from the previous night cancelling our session. I feel grateful that I had checked my phone before driving into Glasgow, grateful to have more time with Mum.

The inner warmth of happiness spreads through my body, and I know it was the best thing for me that the session was cancelled. Somehow, I realise I was not meant to have read the message until I did. Life was giving me the opportunity to see how I would respond to the last minute change. My immediate acceptance showed me the value of my inner work of self-awareness and emotional purification. In the past, I would have berated myself for not looking at my phone sooner and been angry at Yvonne for cancelling.

Misplaced Anger

The ego mind is angry when it doesn't get what it wants when it wants it.

Anger can be a difficult emotion to understand and deal with. For some of us, it is an emotion we have learnt to suppress. For others, it is the emotion we have learned to express, albeit unskilfully. Both approaches generate problems at an individual and collective level. The inappropriate suppression and expression of anger has the potential to impact ourselves, and our families and societies, sometimes for generations. It can create war zones within us and between us. The news portrays a world full of conflict and violence— anger manifested.

Anger creates an adrenalin rush that is potentially addictive. It fosters the perception of strength and invincibility, an illusion of control. We unconsciously seek to escape from and mask feelings of insecurity, helplessness, unworthiness, and pain with anger.

Most of us react to others' anger with the stress response, the body's innate fight, flight, freeze or fawn response. We choose one reaction over another, fight over flight, freeze or fawn, depending on our past experiences, our disposition, and the situation.

Anger's Fallout

When we express anger unhealthfully, we often justify the damage we cause by faultfinding: the way politicians govern, how our partner speaks to us, the unrealistic work targets, the demands of home, a four-hour wait at the hospital, bankers' bonuses, the price of petrol. All these emotional triggers are not creating but exposing our anger. Through our reaction to external circumstances, life is showing us the unresolved hurts that we need to address and heal. Else, we stay in a disempowering continuous loop of anger, reaction, and blame.

Similarly, suppressed anger leads to despair. A distressed mind is unable to see a bigger perspective and can become unbalanced.

Revenge vs. Appropriate Anger

Taking revenge can be a way of giving ourselves permission to act out anger in an unskilful way. "You did this to me, so I have the right to do this to you, or someone else." Revenge can escalate the situation. It may increase suffering and distress, create paranoia, and take us further away from our goodness.

Paradoxically, the energy of anger can be a creative force for positive change. Appropriate anger is our inner fire, which can help us stand up for ourselves and cease giving our power to people who cross our healthy boundaries. It ignites us to finally say no to our victim mentality and others' abusive behaviour, follow our dreams, and fight for a cause. When her son, cycling without protective headgear, was severely disabled in an accident, Rebecca Oaten, aka The Helmet Lady, campaigned successfully for six years to enact a compulsory bike helmet law in New Zealand.

Working with Anger: Ours and Others

In addition to emotional release breathing (chapter 10), we can release the physical energy from anger with movement and sound. For instance, you can dance, swim, go for a walk or run; clean the car, the house, or the fridge; chop wood or cut the grass. You can turn a scream into a tone, specifically a vowel sound, that rises from the belly through the body and out of the top of the head. Toning helps release energy, allowing it to move naturally through and out of the body.[2]

You can also learn to work with your anger differently using your awareness.

1. *Stop, look, and listen.* As soon as you are aware that you are irritated or angry, stop what you are doing, saying, and thinking, and take a deep breath. No matter what your mind tells you, even if it believes the anger is justified, stop. This immediately interrupts any escalation in the irritation, and gives you the opportunity to take stock of the circumstances and deal with the anger emotions differently. If you can, walk away from the situation to give yourself space. (Going to the toilet is an option that I have used many times at work.)

2. *Bring your attention into the body.* Slowly count to ten, inhaling deeply, exhaling gradually, with each number. Notice any sensations of tightness, tension, and anxiety. Keep counting slowly and breathing as

deeply as you can. Imagine breathing fresh air into those parts of your body that are tense. Shaking your body also helps release tension.

3. *Become aware of your thoughts.* What story is your mind running with? Is the story fuelling your irritation and justifying your anger? Notice how your anger speaks and what it says. Investigate what your awareness is showing you without judgement, self-pity, and self-righteousness.

4. *Observe how you feel.* If there is little or no change, start counting to ten again with the intention of creating distance from the anger, detaching from any thoughts, and calming down. If feeling agitated, you can go for a walk to physically release the energy from the body. Allowing yourself to cry is also helpful.

5. *Be persistent.* Continue to deep breathe in cycles of ten until you begin to feel calmer. Notice what it takes and how long it takes for you to bring yourself back into a place of less irritation and more self-control.

#

We can release other people's anger as well. Sensitive or empathic people often subconsciously pick up other people's emotions. Empaths can assume the feelings are their own. They are sad when someone is sad, and become annoyed when another is angry. Marie came to see me because she was confused. She was increasingly disgruntled by minor issues at work that she would have normally brushed off. She had recently moved in with a new partner. "Is the irritation you're feeling of late yours or your partner's?" I asked. She was puzzled. She thought because she felt it, it was hers.

One day, while loading up the car together, Marie felt a wave of anger sweep over her. She looked at her partner and saw his seething expression. In our next session, she said it had been a moment of revelation. She no longer felt any irritation, instead her partner was the one now shouting at the neighbours and politicians. She told me, "Your question helped me. I got my Self back and it opened a door for us to discuss his anger."

Noticing that your behaviour or attitude has changed when you are around others can be a clue that you are picking up on other people's feelings—particularly in intimate relationships, crowds and group situations. Becoming aware of the energy you have taken on from others may be enough to release it. If you are still carrying others' emotions, you can work with your breath to let go of others' energy.

#

Working with Fear

In this section we focus on another debilitating emotion—fear.

Right now, I feel lost. The effort to connect with my authentic Self seems daunting. I have so many fears and anxieties circling around me that I don't know where to start. I sit and cry and feel sorry for myself. The release of tears settles me. I tell myself that I don't need to resolve everything immediately—only to meet what is happening in the here and now, and trust in the intelligence of life and the wisdom of my soul to bring me the things that will help me awaken, step by step. My job is to work with what life brings to me and what arises within. That is enough. I don't have to go looking for things. I don't have to force anything. I don't have to save the world. I relax. The fear lessens.

Reassessing Fear

By holding onto our fears, we give them credence and the power to influence our life. And this influence can be inherently negative. Fear can limit our behaviour, feed our anxieties, rob us of our dreams, and dampen our spirits. It can breed distrust between us and others. For instance, we can fear other people just because they are different, without any rational reason for our apprehension.

Fear can be used by organisations such as banks, governments, corporations, the media, and by people in our life, to control and manipulate. It is important to be alert to our own fears, as well as those that are externally induced. Fear is a sign to look within. The first step in dealing with fear, is awareness.

A healthy approach is to challenge any fear-based mentality. For example, the poverty mentality is a widespread phenomenon that exploits our fear of scarcity and ignores the abundance we do have. It creates a sense of emptiness and dissatisfaction within us that spurs us into continually striving for more things to fill the inner hollowness and create happiness.

I used to believe that it would be impossible to support myself financially in any way other than with a traditional job. This belief kept me tied to the job market for years until my heart offered me a different way, and I decided to take time-out in 2012.

Deciding to step away from the socially acceptable security of employment has repeatedly challenged me to release my fears and vulnerability around money and the future. Each time these fears surface, I say, "I'm OK. I have the money at the moment and things will work out." And they have. Miracles have happened. People have stepped in and offered me support and my needs were met.

Feeling vulnerable is difficult for the mind. It interprets vulnerability as weakness. Yet, behind vulnerability lies our strength and our gifts.

Our imperfections are the doors to perfection.

Our soul has chosen the imperfections that will lead us to develop our strengths. If we remain frightened of being vulnerable we will find it hard to be authentically strong.

How to Conquer Your Fears

In addition to awareness and direct challenge, here are five ways—using your wisdom mind, heart and intentions—to overcome your fears.

Show appreciation. You can actively work to erase your fear mind-set by appreciating and giving thanks for all that you have. Every night before you go to sleep, express gratitude for that day. Every morning on waking, give thanks for your life and the new day.

Engage your wise mind. Life provides you with opportunities to meet your fears, and to develop skilful means to respond. Reflecting on how you did—without judgement—allows you to adopt the strategies that work best for you. For example, I found it difficult to stand up for myself, especially to authority figures. One day, I consciously chose to face these challenges in ways small (such as asking the barista for a hotter coffee) and large (such as expressing my views to my manager). In the beginning, my anxiety made me loud and aggressive, and unable to listen to the other person's perspective for fear that I would give in. By reflecting and persisting, I learnt to be less defensive, quieter, and more relaxed, and to use humour to defuse a situation. Long-standing fears started to dissipate.

Envision what you want. What is your intention in meeting a fear? In the above example about assertiveness, I wanted to be heard and relaxed while expressing my views. When I concentrated on my aim, it was easier to speak up even though the egoic part of me was still intimidated.

Take the medicine of love. Extend love to your fear. Be respectful and caring of the aspect of you that is frightened. Offer reassurance and love from your heart. It is the absence of qualities such as kindness and love that created the fear. In extending self-love, you become the loving parent to the hurt child who still lives within.

Cultivate positive emotions. Fear has a low vibration, whereas positive emotions, such as gratitude, appreciation, joy, and love, reverberate at a higher level. Individual, positive emotions also add to a less fearful, freer collective consciousness.

Some of us may feel fear and despair about the state of the world and about our life. Some may feed the collective consciousness with anger and fear about the unfairness in our society. Such emotions do not transform our everyday reality. They make it heavier and more difficult to bear, and most of the time, do not lead to positive action. Anger and fear cannot reside in a space of kindness and grace. By generating feelings of gratitude and being kind we create favourable changes within ourselves and in the world. We each need to "do our bit,"[3] to transform the world reality, as spiritual teacher Lorna Byrne says.

Chapter 12

Communicating with Sincerity

Only in relationship can you know yourself, not
in abstraction, and certainly not in isolation.[1]
—Jiddu Krishnamurti, Indian spiritual teacher,
speaker and writer

Experiencing Intimacy

We are social beings, and relationships have the potential for much happiness and much tension, conflict, and hurt. We may have lived through interactions fraught with disrespect, disappointment, insecurity, and abuse—ours and others'. Damaging relationships can leave us in pain for days, months, years, or a lifetime. How many of us heal the hurt from a fractious relationship before engaging in a new romance?

It's summer 2017, and Mum and I are sitting in a café. I tell her how difficult it was for me in childhood with Dad, who was often angry, and with her, quiet and emotionally withdrawn. Mum looks at me, "I wasn't always so reticent."

Suddenly, she has my full attention. I come round and sit beside her and hold her hand. Mum speaks about events from her childhood that she had never shared with anyone. In that moment, all the separation that had existed between us falls away, and unconditional love flows freely. In all my life, this moment is the most precious and sweetest. Mum tells me her miracles are Stewart (my brother) and me, as she thought she would never have children. When we leave the café we hug closely, holding each other with the deepest respect and love. This moment changes everything for us, and another door in my heart swings open.

Moments like that can happen at any time. Events on TV and in films, and time spent with children and animals and in nature may also trigger this experience of a deeper, inner connection, especially if you allow yourself to be with the feelings that are arising. Coming out of the socialised bubbles as your heart opens is a beautiful experience. What moves you?

Stop Taking Things Personally

Many years ago, I was at a wedding reception with my then-husband. We were standing with his work colleagues, and one of the men asked me to dance. I love to dance, but I did not like the music and so, I said, "No." I could see that he was surprised. I explained and said that I would dance with him when the music changed. He ignored what I had said, and asked me again. Again, I said, "No," and repeated the reason. He became agitated and asked a third time. And I said, "No" a third time. Everyone was watching us. He asked again. I considered saying yes to defuse the situation, as was my conditioned habit. That day, something inside of me said, "Don't change your mind to please someone or keep the atmosphere pleasant." I repeated, "No." He asked a fifth time. I shook my head and turned away. When the music changed, I asked him if he would like to dance but unsurprisingly, he said, "No." I walked away.

We get angry or hurt by other people's remarks because we are carrying unresolved hurt from our past. We project the hurt and blame onto others for something we have not reconciled. When we stop taking things personally, we act more from our true Self than the ego self. We are freed emotionally from others and can be more objective in our interactions. Similarly, when people lash out at us, they are doing so from a place of pain.

Balancing Our Feminine and Masculine Sides

Our world is comprised of dualities, such as right and wrong, good and bad, right-brain and left-brain, the haves and the have-nots, positive and negative, light and shadow, black and white, passive and active, us and them. Although the duality at the heart of everything is the authentic Self and the ego self, one of the biggest dichotomies we are all immersed in concerns our feminine and masculine sides.

A human being has two inner polarities. One polarity is linked to a feminine (yin energy), associated with intuition, nurturing, compassion for others, and responsiveness to their needs. The other is attuned to a masculine (yang energy), related to power, focus, action, decisiveness, and to one's own self and life.[2] Irrespective of our gender or sexuality, we have one side that predominates depending on our nature, and egoic self. At different times in our life, we need the feminine power and at other times, the masculine. Neither is better. If we reject one side, we will create an internal imbalance, which is then reflected in our life. Such an imbalance is evident in our planet where the egoic masculine power dominates and the Earth is riddled with disease, environmental destruction, conflict, and unhappiness.

The way to wholeness is to bring balance, harmony, and sincerity within, and then reflect that in the way we lead our life.

As a child, I was a tomboy. My maternal grandpa was a footballer and taught me to kick and header a ball. At primary school, I played football with the boys and never played with dolls or wore a dress. My competitive drive continued through my sporting life as an adult. Through following my heart, my whole manner changed. I am much gentler, softer, and more inclusive and service orientated than before, while also being fully focussed on my spiritual growth. The balance between masculine and feminine qualities has grown organically within me.

In 2017, my feminine side's integration was confirmed during a meditation. In a vision, I saw myself standing in front of a door. I knew I had to open the door, but hesitated. Eventually, I turned the key and pushed open the door. Hundreds of crows followed by hundreds of bats flew out. Then, I stepped into the room. An old woman was sitting in the middle of the room, chained to a chair. Her hair was grey and matted, and her clothes were dirty and dishevelled. She was stooped over, skin and bones, barely able to support her weight.

I took a key out of my heart and unlocked the padlock on the chains immobilising the old woman. I walked slowly around the chair unravelling the chains, freeing her. Instinctively, I knew the old woman was me—the Divine feminine aspect of myself that I was freeing. As the old woman stood up slowly from the chair, I held her. We walked out of the room and into a sacred healing pool with a waterfall. I knew that I needed to take the old woman into the waterfall. At first, I thought the flow would be too strong for her, but the water fell gently on us. As I looked at the old woman, she transformed into a beautiful, young maiden, and we embraced and merged into one. It was so touching as I reunited with this once-enfeebled feminine aspect of myself.

Learning from Others

In her groundbreaking book *Embraced by the Light*, Betty J. Eadie wrote about her near-death experience and gaining a different perspective of life on Earth while in the spirit realm. In one scene, she was shown two friends in the spirit world who had decided to incarnate. One friend, who wanted to learn about love, became a banker, and the other, who agreed to help him, became a homeless man. Every day, the banker passed his friend in the street and the homeless man tried to get his friend's attention to elicit his help so that his friend's heart would open.[3] The homeless man was the banker's teacher.

In 2011 I trained as a water pourer, the person who facilitates sweat lodge ceremonies. The sweat lodge is an ancient ceremony once common in indigenous cultures. Participants offer prayers and blessings for themselves and for those who have graced their life, whilst the heat facilitates the release of physical and emotional toxins. In the Native

American Sun Bear tradition I trained in, there are five prayer rounds: a welcome round and then a round that honours each of the directions east, south, west and north. During the south round, we give thanks for all of our relationships.

We start with those with whom we have a loving and supportive relationship, and then thank those with whom we have difficulties. Often, it is only in retrospect that we can see how the difficult people have also helped us to grow. In this way, we honour everyone who has been in our life, and make peace with our past.

With painful events, we strive to come to a place of acceptance and greater understanding. In time these experiences can become gifts for our personal growth. It may take a relationship break-up, an unexpected death, an angry boss, the loss of a job, an illness, or an accident to wake us up and see things clearly as they are. Experiencing any difficulty may be a signal to pay attention to life's messages. Ask, "What is this situation showing me about myself?"

In 2009, while I was living with my parents, my dad accused me of putting something down the bathroom sink that blocked it. I said that I had not done it, but he refused to believe me. I was perplexed and angry. Instead of becoming defensive I told Dad why I was angry with him, which went beyond the current situation. That day, I ended years of disempowerment and lack of self-respect.

After I stood up to my dad, my mind and body were completely relaxed. I felt no guilt for expressing my anger in a constructive and assertive way, nor did I feel any need to apologise to dad as I did in the past. Instead, I gently stood my ground. Weeks passed, and we did not speak.

Christmas Eve, Mum asked me if I would make up with Dad for Christmas day. I said, "No." I explained that this was about me holding self-respect. I knew if I gave in to appease Mum, I would continue to invite people into my life who disrespect me. I had to break the pattern, and Dad's behaviour was helping me do this. Mum understood.

In January, Dad helped me move into a flat in Glasgow. He offered, and I accepted. In that moment, he released his stubbornness and we met as equals. The dynamic of our relationship had shifted, and we both knew it. Before he died, Dad told me how much he admired me. Dad's gift to me was the opportunity to speak my truth, and to reclaim my power and self-respect. I am grateful to him for being the catalyst for this soul lesson.

When Dad and I were not speaking, I was sending him love instead of fuelling the situation with angry thoughts about his unfair behaviour. I did not want conflict between us. Life had shown me repeatedly that giving in did not change anything with Dad. Not dealing with the issue with Dad in the first place had taken me into relationships and even ordinary interactions where I ceded power. It was time to unlearn that behaviour.

Sometimes doing the right thing for our authentic Self, can be arduous. We can also appear heartless to other people who are accustomed to us behaving in a particular way, or who are unaware of the personal process we are going through. Maintaining a spiritual practice that connects us with our authentic Self, a resource that sustains us, can help. Meditation and being in nature provide us with a refuge of calmness.

Healing our relationships involves primarily self-healing. When we become more sincere in our communication with ourselves and others, we overcome the internalised patterns that maintain separation, and more light and happiness come into our life.

Our Job is to Heal Ourselves

In our personal work, we learn to differentiate between what is and is not our responsibility. It is not our job to fix other people. Interfering in the lives of others or allowing ourselves to be manipulated into doing their bidding is another way the programming derails us from walking our path.

A client Sandra complained about her brother's drinking. Every day, he drank alcohol until he blacked out. His flat was a mess, and he refused to clean or cook for himself. Sandra went round to her brother's place daily, cleaned up and made dinner. She admitted that she also brought him booze, because she believed the alcohol kept him alive.

As one of my teachers often said, "Let people do what they do." We are not responsible for their choices and behaviour. We do not know the karmic interplays we are impeding and the potential karma we are creating for ourselves with unrequested interventions or acceding to others' manipulations.

So, when is it appropriate to step in? One night, a friend, Barbara, was taking the bus home. Every seat was taken, and people were standing in the aisle. Three stops before Barbara's, a young woman got on the bus followed by a man who was obviously drunk. As the bus moved, he held onto the post to keep his balance. Then to Barbara's horror, the drunk man started rubbing his butt against the young woman. Offended, the young woman could not move away. As the man continued to rub himself against the young woman, Barbara could feel herself becoming more agitated, but she, too, had gone into freeze mode. Then a man got up, took the drunk man by the hand, guided him to his vacated seat, and stood beside him. Barbara felt relieved and as people got up to leave, they thanked the man who had given up his seat.

The man on the bus saw something inappropriate, and his heart motivated him to act. He did not act out of guilt or judgement, but out of kindness and compassion.

Exercise 3. Sincere Communication

To help you become more self-aware and honest in your communication.

1. Pause now and write down any interactions with others in which you were insincere.

2. As you write, reflect on the situation. Ask, "What prevented me from being honest?" "Do I want to act differently?" If so, "What would help me be authentic?"

As you continue to note and examine your interactions, over time, you will recognise the ways in which you are growing, changing, and learning. Having these honest conversations with yourself can show you where you create problems during your exchanges with others. Sincere communication is another key component for awakening. By opening the doors that our programming keeps hidden and locked, we heal from within.

Chapter 13

Deferring to
Our Wisest Teacher

The wise teacher exists within us. In order to find
this teacher, we need to look inside.
—Fotoula Adrimi, a channeling from ISIS,
the Divine Mother of All

I answer the phone. A representative from my broadband
provider is asking me questions about my internet connection
and computer. I notice my body is becoming agitated as he
speaks. I am bewildered by what he's saying and he's becoming
more demanding. Something does not feel right. I ask to
speak to his supervisor, and another man comes on the line.
As he starts talking, my body begins to shake. I hang up,
and call my internet provider's customer service number. The
operator confirms the call was a scam and that I did the
right thing by not giving out my account information and
ending the call. I thank my body for its reaction and message.

When we live in the present moment, fully in our body and
engaged with our heart and feelings, we have access to

information, understanding, and wisdom from within. Our authentic Self often communicates with us through our body in the form of a hunch, niggle, instinct, intuition, and inner knowing. Yet, if we are disconnected from our body, then we are also cut off from this inner wisdom or dismiss its clues.

How well we adapt to our body can have repercussions for our life and mental health. Women and increasingly, men can feel tremendous pressure to conform to body images portrayed in the media. Even the most beautiful person may be critical of the shape of their nose or the width of their ankles. We may feel gender dysmorphia due to the dominant patriarchal and heterosexual perspectives.

The body has been crucial in my journey of awakening. It is my compass, my guide to negotiate life. The body's inner knowing is ahead of my egoic mind, steering me towards what supports my awakening and away from impediments to my soul's growth. Research by Lisa Feldman Barrett, PhD, an American neuroscientist and professor of psychology, supports my experience of the body's wisdom. She argues that the brain's main purpose is to interpret the body's perceptions.[1] In other words, the body responds first and then the brain engages other bodily communication systems. This body-brain connection is validated in the co-regulation scientific studies by the psychiatrist Martha G. Welch and internal medicine physician Robert J. Ludwig.[2]

The body is also the storehouse of all the issues we need to release in order to awaken. While the mind is fearful of what our personal work may unearth, our body has been holding these issues drama-free all our life, waiting patiently to reveal its lessons and gifts. When we continue to surrender to the wisdom of the body, it will light a path towards union with our Divine Self.

Awakening through the Body

In *The Golden Book of Wisdom*, my colleague Fotoula Adrimi speaks about how, before we are born, we design our body. And that it contains all the karma and conditions our soul has chosen to work through in this lifetime, as well as all the wisdom and gifts that we will need to fulfil our life's purpose.[3] To awaken, we need to face, acknowledge, and uproot all the layers of conditioning and karma that our body is carrying. This means purifying our entire body, all the way into the cells.

We may have already dealt with some of the issues our body carried, whilst other issues may be unknown, biding their time until we are ready to discover them. Some physical conditions may never manifest, unless we deviate wildly from our soul's chosen path. Illness may be the soul's way of helping us realign with our purpose for incarnating. Mark, a client, gave up his spiritual path and healing practice, as his partner Sue was fearful of alternative spirituality. He grew depressed, finding little joy in his everyday life. After years of suppressing the wishes of his soul, Mark developed fibromyalgia and was in constant pain. Mainstream medicine had little more to offer than painkillers. One day, a friend suggested he try spiritual healing. Mark noticed that during the healing sessions, he was pain free and resumed his dedication to his spiritual path.

Earthing in Nature

When we are ungrounded and not fully present in our body, we can become confused, disorientated, and lack direction.

In the same vein, if we have a spiritual practice that regularly lifts us out of the lower states of consciousness into higher vibrations, we also need some way of coming back fully into our body. Contact with the natural world is a quick way of grounding and bringing the spiritual into the physical.

Since 2010, a growing body of scientific research is showing that grounding, or earthing, can have remarkable health benefits, including reduced pain and inflammation; improved sleep and blood circulation; eased skin rashes; and increased mobility. When skin contacts the earth, the body is connected to a rich supply of negatively charged free ions. These ions have been shown to help our physical body rebalance its systems and energy fields by synchronising our internal biological clocks; neutralising the harmful effects of exposure to certain domestic appliances, such as microwaves, and external electromagnetic energy fields, such as mobile phone towers and Wi-Fi; and stabilising physiological and hormonal rhythms.[4]

We are part of nature, and thus, can benefit from being in nature.

Any skin contact with the earth is potent, but the best way is to walk barefoot. Reflexology asserts that our feet have more nerve endings and more receptivity and discharge points than any other part of the body. Our whole anatomy is reflected in the feet.[5]

Releasing Trauma

Different people come into our life at particular times to offer guidance and help. It is life's way of supporting us. In

2014, in a workshop in Kathmandu, Nepal, I met a yoga practitioner named Joe. One day, Joe was speaking about a particular yogic breathing technique that caught my attention. Normally, I meditate with my tongue at the roof of my mouth.

According to Chinese medicine, the two master meridians, or energy channels, in the body start at the perineum, the area in men between the anus and scrotum, and in women, between the anus and vulva. The yang (male) meridian, called the "governing vessel," travels up the back of the body through the bony tissues of the spinal column, over the skull bones, to the roof of the mouth. The yin (female) meridian, known as the "conception vessel," travels up the front of the body, through the soft tissues, and ends at the tip of the tongue.[6] When we meditate with the tip of the tongue on the roof of the mouth, we complete this primary meridian circuit, which enables energy to flow freely within the body.

In the technique Joe spoke about, the tongue is pushed as far back as possible in the mouth. Curious, I tried the technique and after a few weeks during my meditations, my jaw started to shake. If I moved my tongue to my normal position in the roof of my mouth, the shaking stopped. According to the trauma release work of David Berceli, known as TRE, one way for trauma to leave the body is through shaking.[7] The new tongue placement, by inducing involuntary shaking, was helping me release unknown trauma from the body.

Suggestion: If you meditate, you can try both of these tongue placement techniques and see what happens for you.

Exercise 4. De-stressing the Body by Shaking

To help you release tension and stress from your body.

1. Play any vibrant piece of music, such as the fifteen-minute shaking track from the Osho Kundalini Meditation CD by Deuter, or shake in silence.

2. Stand with your legs shoulder width apart, eyes open or closed, and arms hanging loosely by your side. Notice how you are feeling.

3. Bring your focus into your body as you take three deep breaths in and out. Take your awareness into your feet and feel the connection between your feet and the floor.

4. Intend to shake out all the tension and tightness from your body. Feel where the body wants to release any pressure, and start shaking, allowing your body to direct the movement. Let the shaking travel through your whole body—feet, legs, torso, arms, and head. Keep shaking for fifteen minutes.

5. Slowly come to a place of stillness. Sit or lie down in silence for five minutes.

6. Notice how your body and mind feel.

It is important to shake for a minimum of fifteen minutes to allow the body time to release the tension. Ignore any attempts by the mind to shorten the exercise.

Following Our Inner Compass

In 2004, the stress of a relationship break-up, combined with studying for my final university BSc (psychology) exams and looking for employment, severely impacted my health. By the time I saw my doctor, I was very ill. I was trembling uncontrollably; my hair was falling out; I had heart palpitations; my ankles were swollen; and I was losing weight despite eating twice as much as usual. I was mentally agitated and in emotional turmoil—constantly on the verge of tears. My doctor diagnosed hyperthyroidism, which a blood test confirmed. I was relieved to have a diagnosis, but shocked and frightened that I had distressed my body to such an extent.

The doctor prescribed Carbimazole and referred me to a thyroid consultant at a local hospital, who added thyroxine. The consultant would try to stabilise my condition by finding the right dosages of both drugs. If after a year I showed no improvement, my thyroid would be rendered inactive through radioactive iodine and I would be on thyroxine for the rest of my life. I was horrified.

The thought of being dependent on a prescription drug for the rest of my life was incomprehensible. Determined to take responsibility for my health, I did my own research.

I continued with the Carbimazole, which I could feel was helping me. I did not take the prescribed thyroxine tablets. My instinct was that once my condition had stabilised through the Carbimazole and alternative treatments, I could gradually reduce the Carbimazole. This would allow my body to slowly heal itself. I had acupuncture treatments, and took homeopathic remedies and vitamins and mineral supplements. I worked with an applied kinesiologist who helped me rebalance my mental and emotional systems. I read Louise Hay's book *You Can Heal Your Life*,[8] and recited the hyperthyroidism affirmation many times each day.

After five months, I went back to my doctor and explained my plan to heal myself. She agreed to support me and suggested more frequent blood tests to monitor my hormone levels. She also said that I needed to tell the consultant, which I did on my next hospital visit. I was immediately met with the consultant's fear that manifested as a threat. She said that my approach would not work and in six months, I would be pleading with the hospital to take me back and by then, the waiting list would be full. Hit by her fear, I felt shaken but held firm.

By the end of the first year, I had slowly reduced the Carbimazole from five tablets a day to three. My blood test showed that although my thyroid was still overproducing hormones, my body had gone into a negative feedback loop, a compensatory self-regulatory system. Consequently, my overall hormone levels were normal. My doctor was pleasantly surprised. Instinctively, I could feel that my body and I were working in tandem.

Over the next nine months, I gradually stopped the alternative treatments, and I reduced the Carbimazole from three tablets to zero. By the end of the second year, I was drug-free, my body had returned to its usual positive feedback loop, and my hormone levels were normal. After two years, I had healed myself from what the consultant described as an "irreversible illness." I felt validated and empowered.

This health crisis was an important initiation for me. Here is what I learned. Accept the diagnosis. Take responsibility for the treatment process. Trust your instincts and your body's wisdom. Utilise the power of your mind to focus on what you want. Find a network of people to support you. Explore the treatment options. Know that you can heal you.

Befriending What Is

In his bestselling book *The Power of Now*, Eckhart Tolle writes, "Whatever the present moment contains, accept it as if you had chosen it. Always work with it, not against it. Make it your friend and ally, not your enemy. This will miraculously transform your whole life."[9]

When something happens to you, you have two choices: befriend the situation or rail against it. The longer acceptance takes, the more distress you generate for yourself. In contrast, by befriending the circumstances you encounter, you shift your attitude, and open the door to transformation.

Acceptance can also be offered to events and decisions from your past. Regardless of the decisions you made, even if they did not work out as you would have hoped or expected, it is important to respect them. Let the befriending release you from any guilt, regret, disappointment, and self-criticism you are still carrying.

Taking Care of the Body

In addition to earthing, shaking, and befriending, we can pursue other actions to care for our body, and build a meaningful connection with this pillar of wisdom. Your body, your ally.

Pay attention to the body's signals. The body is continually providing you with information about what's happening internally and externally. Listen.

Laugh more. Laughing is a quick way to relax. As Mark Twain said, "Against the assault of laughter nothing can stand."[10] Laughter benefits us physically, psychologically, and spiritually. Think about something that makes you laugh and start laughing. It could be anything—a funny scene in a movie, a joke, something you witnessed.

Move your body. The body loves being active. You could dance, walk, swim, run, or attend a gym class. You could use a practice that combines focussed breathing, awareness, and movement such as yoga, tai chi, qigong, or the five Tibetan rites. A friend, Adrienne, walks her dog twice daily. It is her spiritual practice, a time to connect with nature, to enjoy being quiet, to have fun with her dog, and be physically active.

Eat and drink what your body needs to be well. Ask your body, "What do you need to be healthy?" Attend to what it says. Notice how the body responds to the changes you make. Homeopathy may also help you clear the body from the accumulated pollutions and heavy metals.

Breathe deeply. Conscious breathing connects us into the body immediately. A few deep breaths every hour will help you relax and build your relationship with your body. Try this: consciously take a slow, deep breath in. And then, gradually exhale. Pay attention to the entire exhale. Pause. Repeat four times. Slow, conscious exhales engage our parasympathetic nervous system (PNS), and the PNS automatically relaxes us.[11]

Experience physical touch. Hug your body. Hug a friend. Treat yourself to a massage. Physical touch has the capacity to heal and redce anxiety and stress.

In these ways, you can learn to look after your body in a more germane way; build a healthy connected relationship with your body; utilise the body's inherent healing ability; and, create a strong physical container that will support your awakening process.

PART IV

NOURISHING THE SOUL: THE SPIRIT

Chapter 14

Integrating the Unconscious

We can hardly bear to look. The shadow may carry
the best of the life we have not lived. Go into the
basement, the attic, the refuse bin. Find gold there.
Find an animal who has not been fed or watered.
It is you!! This neglected, exiled animal, hungry
for attention, is a part of your self.[1]
—Marion Woodman, Canadian author, poet
and psychoanalyst

I am sitting in my hall, my back propped against the wall. I am frightened and want to run away. I know there is something within that I have to face. I take a deep breath and focus in my heart to steady myself. I tell myself everything is OK. No one needs to know what I will discover and life already knows. It is me who is in the dark, hiding from myself. As I start to feel the fear, my body shakes and my mind becomes agitated. I continue to breathe slowly and affirm, "Everything is OK." I say to the fear, "Tell me what this is about." Gradually, a familiar story unfolds. Knowing the story is not enough, I have to go deeper and acknowledge what lies underneath the story—the part I have been running from. I face and accept for the first time something I did that I am not proud of.

Tears flow as the hurt, shame, fear, guilt, and sadness manifest in my body. All the emotions I have kept hidden, not wanting to feel, not wanting to own, I now set free. I stay with them all as I shake and breathe their energy through and out of my body. After a while, the tears and sensations cease and I continue to sit, breathing into my body, resting now in the stillness. "You did it," my heart tells me, "You faced your fear. Well done for not running from what is inside you." My journey with the shadow had begun.

\#

In *The Dark Side of the Light Chasers*,[2] self-help author Debbie Ford speaks beautifully about uncovering our shadow. Each of us has aspects of ourselves that we like and acknowledge— our light side—and aspects that we may not like or know about—our shadow side. The shadow projects and plays name, shame, and blame. It is a significant and traumatising aspect of the human experience. We all project, and are affected by it when we take others' projections personally. Rather than behaving in accord with the shadow's moods and demands, we need to embrace and integrate all its aspects and heal it so that we are no longer influenced by its wiles.

Understanding Projection to Uncover Our Shadow

Ford states that projection is a common process whereby we unconsciously cast or project our perceived flaws onto other people. To illustrate, the teenager afraid to express her own anger will see people acting aggressively all around her. The woman who lacks self-respect will accuse her family of being uncaring. The husband considering having an affair will fear his wife is unfaithful. The executive who loses a business deal will complain about her colleague's stupidity. In the phenomena of projection, the things we say to others are often the things we need to take heed of. The judgements we direct at others can be our hidden self-criticisms.

According to the American author and psychologist Ken Wilbur, projection is easy to identify. Most emotional responses indicate that we are projecting. For example, if we are walking down the street and become annoyed at a passerby littering, then we are projecting. If, on the other hand, we notice but choose to not react, then there is no projection. In this way, awareness of our emotional reactions to situations and people can be a catalyst for personal growth.

When many of our actions are unconscious, we can become indignant, confused, and irritated by our experiences, and annoyed with life for what we perceive as unfair and unjust. Projection is another way for life to help us to awaken. The situations and people we encounter are a mirror for our unconscious attitudes and actions.

For example, I began to monitor what qualities I was complaining about in others. I noticed I was judging one of my friends for being irritable. Eventually I turned it around and asked, "What am I grumpy about?" Then I realised I was annoyed that a reimbursement for a cancelled flight was delayed. As I discovered the cause of days of irritability, I burst out laughing and released the irritation.

Welcoming Our Shadow and Light

Unconsciously, our shadow can direct our reactions and reactive patterns at events and people. When we are attracting a particular personality type, we can welcome the insight as a signal: to address unresolved issues, we attract our opposite. Victim personalities attract master personalities—until they stand up for themselves. People pleasers are often drawn to the emotionally unavailable, till they learn to look after their own needs instead of everyone else's.

Until we resolve the underlying patterns we carry, we will be drawn to the same type of challenging situations and people. I was once the line-manager for a team of therapists. For three years, I was regularly confronted with issues from the therapists, project manager, and office staff. When I took a step back and reframed each challenge as an opportunity to address an issue within myself, I was able to be more effective and helpful to myself and the other person. Even in the less fruitful encounters, I learned something. Afterwards, I would ask myself, "What happened? How could I have handled the situation better?"

The human part of me wants an easy life, conflict-free, whereas my soul knows that I am here to grow and develop. These exchanges are doors towards self-realisation, and it takes time and effort to walk through them in a good way. The question becomes, "Can I set aside the human part and see these issues for the lessons they are in the bigger picture of my soul development?"

Acknowledging our goodness with grace is just as important as facing those aspects of ourselves that we may find disagreeable. Sometimes, we can find it difficult to honour our worth. People may refute compliments as soon as they are expressed. Learning to accept sincere praise supports us to strengthen our good points and nourish our soul. At the same time, we can actively work to uncover and change those traits and behaviours that unnerve us.

We need to integrate both our light and shadow in order to find a balanced way of being, lessen our fear of intimacy, and deepen our connection to our true nature: love. This is the work that opens our heart so that we can establish a healthier relationship with ourselves, those around us, and life itself.

The Space in My Hall

For six years whenever I needed to process something, positive and negative, I retreated to a particular place in my hall. I gave myself the time and space to sit and connect inside, to feel whatever emotions came up—embarrassment, fear, anger, hurt, disappointment, joy, excitement.

This personal processing time was important for me in many ways. I developed and strengthened self-trust and fostered greater self-care. I better understood the human predicament and the conditioning. I contemplated unresolved situations and faced feelings that lay trapped inside, sometimes for decades. In time, I became less fearful and learned that it was OK to own and accept all my actions, feelings, and thoughts. I opened up to who I am in the moment—light and shadow—and developed self-compassion and self-forgiveness. In that space, I became a good friend to myself.

Staying with the Good

I also chose to feel the positive emotions that arose. My usual strategy when I became aware of a positive feeling, such as happiness, was to not fully engage and quickly continue with whatever I was doing. As I took the time to experience happiness, something beautiful happened. The happiness grew into joy, and I would sit and experience joy in my body. This unsettled my conditioned Scottish outlook of doom and gloom. I could feel the pull of distraction from the happy feeling into negativity. "It won't last, so what's the point in experiencing it?" To counter this, I offered joy to the despondent part.

Instinctively, I knew staying with the good was important for my well-being. In allowing the positive emotions to be in my body, I could change the chemistry of my body, and gradually neutralise the toxicity of years of stress, tension, and anxiety.[3] I imagined the positivity flowing into every cell of my body, and would stay in that space for as long as I could. In this way, I was acknowledging and connecting with my essence: the living light that I am. I was allowing myself to be this light and this light to reorient my body's chemistry and dissolve the shadows. The more I allowed myself to experience positive states, the longer I was able to stay in them and the less agitated the egoic part became. Experiencing the positive helps us to rediscover and reclaim the goodness we felt as children. Happiness and joy are our prerogative.

Exercise 5. Accepting Your Goodness

To help you embrace the qualities of your authentic Self.

1. Write down, or consciously note, the qualities that you admire in other people as they occur.

2. For each quality, ask yourself, "How does this quality manifest in me?" Do not let your mind override or dismiss what your wise Self says.

#

Not everyone's circumstances allow them to sit and work through their issues in the way I did in my hall; however, there are many ways to become self-aware and, more importantly, action our intention. If our intention is for personal growth, then we can ask, "What am I doing about it?" Ellie, a client and single mother of two, intended to have more time for herself. We explored what was stopping her from taking me time. After three months of counselling, Ellie introduced clearer boundaries with her children, which supported her intention to value herself. Ellie's self-esteem increased and her relationship with her children changed. Their attitude towards their mum became more positive and supportive.

The life circumstances we each experience can help us develop awareness and grow consciously. No one's life is necessarily any better or easier than any other. We may think that the grass is greener for another person, but how would we know? We can only live our life and start where we are, to paraphrase Buddhist teacher and nun Pema Chödrön. In doing so, we honour the situations that our soul has chosen to experience in this lifetime and the decisions we have made along the way.

Chapter 15

A Journey from Mind to Heart

Open your eyes to the beauty around you,
open your mind to the wonders of life, open your
heart to those who love you, and always be true
to yourself.[1] —Maya Angelou, American poet,
author, and civil rights activist

It is my first medicine walk and I am anxious. The medicine walk is a ceremony where participants walk in nature to see what the natural world reflects back to them. The reflection is the medicine. Most medicine walks start at sunrise and end at sunset. In this extended ceremony, participants are staying out for forty-eight hours, alone and without food. After four hours of searching for a spot to pitch my tarpaulin, I still cannot decide. Finally, in desperation, as the light fades and the rain starts, I choose a place on a slope between two trees. By the time I put up the tarpaulin and slip into my sleeping bag, it is dark. Two moths land on my outstretched hand and stay with me for most of the night. I take comfort in their presence and finally relax. In the morning, I watch the canvas of nature turn from grey to a kaleidoscope of pink, orange, blue, and yellow as the sun rises over the mountains. It is mesmerising. I had no idea the sun colours our world so dramatically.

The remainder of the time out, I embrace the natural world around me—the plants, trees, birds, and other wildlife. Despite the relentless rain, my shelter stays dry thanks to the slope and waterproof tarp. I return to base camp in a state of joy, and we each share the story of our experiences. Brigitte, our guide, asks me to title my story. The words come unbidden: "A Journey from Mind to Heart." This is my medicine from the walk.

I Am Love, Love Is Who I Am

In 2007, I discovered something that helped me become kinder and more loving towards myself. Following a meditation practice, the phrase "I am love, love is who I am" popped into my awareness. For the next three months, at the end of my meditation practice, I added a short exercise. I said the phrase "I am love, love is who I am" with sincerity, and then waited for a little while, feeling into my body. I repeated the exercise four times.

At first, my mind resisted, throwing up negative thoughts (I am foolish, I am crazy), and rational reasons to give up (I don't have time, nothing's happening). I ignored both. Part of me was curious (What will happen if I continue?). I had read many times that "Love is the answer, we are love, love conquers all," and I wanted to discover for myself if it is true. I challenged myself to prove the power of love.

After a week, as I meditated in the silence after saying the phrase, I felt a warm sensation arising in my heart area that gradually spread throughout my body. In response, I focussed in my heart centre as I repeated the phrase. Each day, the warmth emerged—sometimes quickly, sometimes slowly, sometimes deeply, sometimes fleetingly. The quality of the feeling—soft, open, warm, and gentle—remained the same. It did not ask anything of me. There was no story attached. And nothing for me to do. It was just there to experience. I felt spacious and calm, more accepted, and loved. A lightness arose in my being that was peaceful.

My body loved the release. My mind was amazed. And the part of me that I now know as the authentic Self, felt validated. With continued practice, I was softening not only during the meditation space, but also in my daily life. I felt relaxed and comfortable with myself and more at ease around others. Spontaneously and having shed my shyness, I would offer small acts of kindness.

I then began repeating the mantra outside meditation. It was another way to reconnect with my Self and bring in softness and warmth to offset any accumulated tension and anxiety. I was slowly and quietly learning to love and respect myself. The proof was my growing self-esteem. As further confirmation, friends also commented on the changes in me.

The impact of the mantra was so positive that its influence organically extended into other areas of my life. It was as if my inner world was directing me into another, more natural way of being. I brushed my teeth and hair with more awareness and care. I became more intimate with and kinder to my body. After a shower, I would gently massage cream into my skin. As I hugged my body, I told it how much I appreciated and loved it. All the while, I ignored any negative mind talk that found fault with a particular body part or laughed at me when I kissed my arms and hands. (Kissing and hugging your body is a great way to show love to yourself.) I did not let the mind chatter stop my practice of self-nurturance. Intuitively, I knew what I was doing was important.

What ways can you extend love to yourself? Try using the phrase "I am love, love is who I am." Try kissing your hand now. Notice if your mind dismisses the idea.

Slowing Down and Taking in More

As a consequence of my growing self-love, I also slowed down and stopped rushing. I gave up running for buses, hurrying to appointments, squeezing in more in a day by multitasking. As my mind pressed me to accelerate, I chose to stroll, breathe consciously, and release any discomfort about my new approach. I was inviting my mind to unlearn the old pattern of adrenaline-induced tension and learn self-respect.

It was a relief to release the self-imposed pressure to be industrious. Paradoxically, even though I have continued with self-love and slowing down, my life is still busy. How is that possible? By increasing my awareness and living more consciously, I sense more and my life is fuller. My mind is calmer and more focussed. I seldom procrastinate and am less distracted, thus more effective and efficient. And I now also instinctively prioritise, which procrastination had prevented. My inner intelligence has blossomed and coordinated my life in a more streamlined way than my mind ever had.

Transmuting Insecurity with Kindness

David R. Hawkins, an American psychiatrist, physician, and spiritual teacher, wrote, "Simple kindness to one's self and all that lives is the most powerful transformational force of all. It produces no backlash, has no downside, and never leads to loss or despair."[2]

In 2011, I was in Glastonbury with friends. Guided by our unseen helping spirits, we found a small standing stone once used by pilgrims as a gateway into Glastonbury. Our spirit guides asked us to listen to the message that the stone had for each of us.

At the time, I found such tasks daunting. I was being asked to engage my sixth sense perception and relax my left-brain thinking. Almost immediately, resistance and fear manifested, reinforcing "my no can do belief." When it was my turn with the stone, I was filled with agitation. A flood of insecurity and doubts surfaced. Even though I could feel a surge of energy from the stone, my mind was in panic mode. The thought of getting a message and getting the right message filled me with fear and dismay.

I was stunned by my mind's reaction. It had been a long time since my self-critic was so vicious and judgemental. I was also embarrassed by my inability to listen. I stepped away from the stone, and some of the stress abated. I would have to try again. With my friends' encouragement, I returned. Again, all the negativity arose, but amazingly, this time, I heard a single word clear as a bell. From habit, my mind dismissed it, so again, with my friends' support, I stayed at the stone until my mind had relaxed enough to allow me to accept the word I had heard: Hat-Hor.

(The ancient Egyptian goddess Hat-hor is the Divine Mother of unconditional love who nurtures all beings.)

Although I eventually accomplished the task, my mind continued to criticise my perceived ineptitude. For the rest of the day, self-recrimination and despondency hung over me like a black cloud. That night, I spoke with my friends about what had happened and how I felt. One friend suggested that I extend kindness and love to the part of me that had been so frightened. Even with years of inner work, we can succumb to situations and forget what we have learned. This is the natural ebb and flow of the journey of awakening. Caught up in the fear this event induced, I had forgotten how to be kind to myself.

For the next two days, I continued to bring in kindness, love, and gentleness to my mind each time the residue from the experience appeared. Like earthquakes in the natural world, when we face a challenging experience, we also have to cope with any aftershocks. I imagined my insecurity as a baby that I was holding with kindness. I spoke reassuringly to it, "It's all OK, little one. It's just fear and doubt coming up because of the increased awareness. There's nothing wrong with being afraid. Breathe it out. Let it go." My mind quieted and the fear lessened and eventually left.

Try speaking kindly to yourself when you are experiencing difficulties. The more kindness and love you can offer yourself in tough times, the easier it can be to move through the difficulty. When you flood yourself with love, you transmute the negative energy. As you move towards the light of your heart, you gradually overcome the mind's pessimistic tendencies.

Accepting Good Support

My friends' help was invaluable. No matter how much self-awareness we develop, seeing beyond our familiar issues and usual defences can be hard. The outside perspective and support of a partner, friend, colleague, or therapist in helping us address problems can be valuable.

Asking for support may be difficult for us. Perhaps we think seeking help means admitting failure and is a sign of weakness. Maybe we are frightened of experiencing vulnerability and exposing ourselves as imperfect. Many of us turn away from or refuse help when we most need it. The more aware we are about needing help and allowing support, the greater our chances of easing pain and discomfort.

Elevating Our Consciousness through Gratitude

The heart generates the most energy in the body and thus, is our richest energy resource. The article "Neuroscience Reveals: Gratitude Literally Rewires Your Brain to Be Happier" cites several scientific studies that show heartfelt gratitude raises our feelings of positivity and physical well-being. It elevates us out of the lower frequencies of doubt, anxiety, fear, and worry.[3] Consciously generating feelings of gratitude and appreciation throughout our day can gradually change our relationship with ourselves, life, and everyone around us.

Dr Valerie V. Hunt was the first scientist to measure human energy fields. Her research demonstrated that when individuals experience elevated states of consciousness, such as gratitude and love, they access higher insights and transcendental ideas.[4]

In these exalted states, people acquired information that they had no conscious knowledge of. This is the wisdom of the awakened state, the wisdom that lies within your heart centre and is accessible to you.

Exercise 6. Generating Gratitude

To help you raise your vibration and enhance your mood.

1. Sit quietly for five minutes. Close your eyes, and gently focus your attention on your breath.

2. Allow the breath to take your awareness into your body. With each in-breath, intend to bring all your energy into your body. With each exhale, focus in your heart centre.

3. When your mind and body feel calmer, keep your attention in your heart centre. Intend to generate feelings of gratitude and appreciation. Say "thank-you" three times, and then focus on the actual feelings of gratitude generated by your intention. When the feelings of appreciation arise, stay with them and allow the feelings to grow and expand. If your attention drifts to thoughts or stories, gently bring it back to the heart and the sensation of gratitude.

4. After a few minutes, when the feeling of gratitude is stronger, intend that the feeling fills every part of your body. Say, "May every cell of my body be filled with and nourished by gratitude."

5. Stay with the experience for ten minutes. Then slowly bring your focus back to your breath and out into the room. Gently open your eyes.

6. Take a moment to become aware of how you feel. Do you feel different from when you began the exercise? If so, in what ways?

Experiencing gratitude is one of the quickest ways to increase your vibration—even to pure states of bliss and joy. The key is to allow yourself to soften and feel the gratitude as a physical sensation.

Chapter 16

Revealing the Divine Self

Michelangelo wrote, "The sculpture is already complete within the marble block, before I start my work. It is already there, I just have to chisel away the superfluous material."[1] Like Michelangelo releasing the statue from within the marble block, our spiritual practice chisels away the conditioning to reveal the authentic Self. Spiritual practice encompasses the ceremonies, meditations, practices, and spiritual initiations that facilitate connection with our Divine Self.

A spiritual initiation is a process of attunement whereby high vibrational energy flows into the body to open our spiritual channels and raise our vibration. Each initiation is only the beginning of the journey. Our spiritual and personal development work has to continue to anchor the higher vibration in the body, so that our body, mind, and nervous system are able to hold any subsequent initiation.[2]

Spiritual teachers tell us that our ultimate soul's purpose is to awaken. The intention is universal at soul level.[3] Some of us may not be aware of this purpose, whilst others may feel an inner calling to explore who we are and follow a spiritual path.

Spiritual practice has been the key to awakening for thousands of years on Earth. We gradually discover that our authentic Self is none other that the eternal Divine light, the living light. Until we awaken, we cannot experience this light fully due to the veils of the conditioning. Even when we read spiritual teachings that say, for example, we are unconditional love, unless we embody this love and express it in our lives, this statement becomes another belief.

We cannot learn about who we are by reading books or listening to lectures alone. The understanding of who we are has to be activated within us. And this activation happens in stages; otherwise, it would be too much for the mind to cope with.

In 2009, when I woke up from the coma, I was a radiant being filled with joy and happiness. This was a cognizance generated through the experience of being awake and being alive without the conditioning.

Building the Inner Foundation

Psychiatrist and author Elisabeth Kübler-Ross said, "People are like stained glass windows. They sparkle and shine when the sun is out, but when the darkness sets in, their true beauty is revealed only if there is a light from within."[4]

Through practices that seek to transform the ego identity, we can connect to a higher realisation and a more encompassing perspective of ourselves and the world. Spiritual practice is like a river that cleanses us, cell by cell, of unhealthy mind-sets and karmic silt. Each time we practice, we dip into this pure river and expand our inner foundation. We quietly erode and discard the patterns, issues, and programmed thoughts that hinder and limit us.

For most of my adult life, each morning upon waking, I would feel a few moments of peace before anxiety surfaced and settled in for the day. In 2015, I noticed that some days the anxiety did not appear until later in the day. In 2016, as I was about to speak in a meditation group on the value of a regular spiritual practice, I realised that the anxiety had vanished. The uneasiness was dissolved through my daily practice.

Without a spiritual practice, it can be difficult to detach from unskilful beliefs. The mind will continue to manipulate and control our life. We will be more likely to create and get caught up in everyday dramas and look for solutions outside of ourselves rather than accessing the wisdom and knowledge that exists within.

First Tastes of Awakening Experiences

People with a regular spiritual practice report blissful experiences of higher consciousness. Such states provide a glimpse of the awakened mind. At that moment, our soul is touched by a universal truth that can be life changing. This is a felt truth that we may not be able to articulate.

This experience is a seed, a small seed of light activated within that is nourished through further practice. The way we each choose to water our seeds is personal. Whatever way you choose, the activation of these seeds is not something you can control; it happens unexpectedly at a particular time for you, according to your soul's plan and personal development path.

Three Ways to Practise

There are three ways to engage in spiritual practice and generate the awakened mind: direct instruction, group practice, and individual immersion.

The traditional way is to work with someone who already has many seeds activated, such as a lama, guru, or awakened teacher. Being within this person's elevated energy field as they teach and facilitate ceremonies can help raise our vibration and create the circumstances for our experience of the awakened mind.

The second way is to practice with a spiritual group, where we cocreate a stronger energy field. The power of the circle can initiate a shift in us. In a group, energy flows from each person into a consolidated vortex of power and light, which then flows back into the group. A circle's power is derived not only from the number but also from the focussed attention of practitioners. The group that remains steady in the energy field benefits all participants.

The third way is to have a personal, daily spiritual practice where we regularly immerse ourselves in practices that strengthen our inner connection. Instead of a guru or group meditation facilitator, we become our own wise teacher.

Regardless of our method(s), we have to maintain self-discipline and concentration. On the path towards awakening, we may get diverted and take the long road round. Losing our way and returning to the path is not a good or bad thing, but a spiritual lesson in itself.

The Difference between Personal Development and Spiritual Practice

Spiritual practice can take many forms, including meditation, yoga, mantra chanting, tai chi, shamanic journeying, qigong, prayer, and ceremonial and ritual experiences from sweat lodges and vision quests to more traditional pujas, Ramadan, and Mass. All these practices are usually undertaken at a specific time, either alone or communally, and have in common the opportunity to celebrate and foster our connection with the Divine. The practices can help purify and release the karma and negative energy stored in the body from this and other lifetimes, as well as ancestral karma. In time, our identity changes and reflects our new inner world.

Personal development is the self-reflective work we do outside spiritual practice, to engage with and resolve recurring issues and unskilful behaviour patterns. For many people, this can be supported by counselling, life-coaching, mindfulness training, journaling, and reading self-help books.

Spiritual practice and personal development are distinct and separate but symbiotic disciplines; their benefits overlap within and outside of the practice sphere. Together, they accelerate our soul's evolution and help us better navigate life. What we learn through our spiritual practice we can take into our everyday life, and vice versa.

Suggestions to Advance Your Progress

Do your spiritual practice with a positive attitude—despite any random thoughts, restlessness, frustration, and physical aches and pains. When judgement and doubts arise, acknowledge the thought and return to your intention. Everything that happens during spiritual practice is part of the growing pains of soul development. It suffices that you make the effort to practice. Even if the mind is lost in thoughts, your soul is benefitting from every spiritual engagement.

In our Western culture of the quick fix, we may become discouraged by our apparent lack of spiritual progress. We may assume the practice is not working, we are not doing it right, or nothing is happening.

Equanimity does not happen overnight, but you can help it along.

- Disregard the mind's judgements.

- Surrender any expectation of what spiritual practice is and any desired outcome. Looking for results limits the power of your practice.

- Express gratitude for all you have and your practices that nourish the authentic Self.

- Persevere. There is no other way.

Awakening is not a commodity; it is a process. We have to transform the ego mind if we wish to awaken to peace, and that takes time and effort.

Transforming the Ego

Wise spirit teachers explain that the aim of spiritual practice and self-development is ego-death. Despite its name, ego-death is not an annihilation, but a transformation from one state of being into another. We transform from the "me" self, the egoic identity of separation, to "all," the expansive awakened state of Oneness. As in physical death, where we leave behind the physical body, the spiritual death of the ego recognises that we leave behind aspects of the social programming that restrain us, so that we can be birthed into higher states of awareness.[5]

So, what does the death of the ego feel like? Most commonly, it is not a violent change but a subtle shift, a staged process—in effect, a lot of little deaths or changes in awareness. This gradual process protects our sanity. Until we wake up, the ego keeps us grounded and safe, so that we can function in the world and look after our needs.

The necessity for the gradual ego transformation is illustrated in a classic, Buddhist story about two frogs. One day, a frog from the ocean travelled inland and came across another frog playing in a small pond. The ocean frog proceeded to tell the pond frog about the vast ocean he came from. The pond frog did not believe that so much water existed. Ocean frog persuaded pond frog to travel back with him to see it. Alas, as pond frog caught sight of the expansiveness of the ocean, his head exploded. The experience was too much for the pond frog's mind to assimilate.

We transform the ego safely by continually immersing ourselves, through spiritual practices, in the light and sacredness of our Divine being. This gradually transmutes the injurious and destructive aspects of the mind and moves us from fear to trust, and from individuality to universal love. In time, we become the pillar of wisdom that holds together the structure of the inner temple.

Psychic Gifts (Siddhis)

Siddhi is a Sanskrit term usually translated as "psychic power." Some people are born with psychic gifts, and for others, the siddhis can open up spontaneously as a result of spiritual and personal development. The most common siddhis are clairvoyance (inner seeing), clairaudience (inner hearing), clairsentience (inner feeling), and clairgnosis (inner knowing). The more advanced siddhis, such as bilocation, levitation, and teleportation, are generally associated with spiritual masters.[6]

The allure of these gifts can derail us from our path if we are not vigilant in our intentions. Our ego can attach to the attention the siddhis garner from others, and we may use them, consciously or unconsciously, for personal gain. Recognise any perceived reward as another stage to be transcended on the way to awakening.

Sacred Sound—Nourishment for the Soul

In ancient Egypt, toning and chanting were used to restore harmony in a person both on a physical and psychological level. This has been borne out by research highlighting the efficacy of music to heal. Studies also show that sound can synchronise our brain waves and create profound states of relaxation, making it possible to access altered states of consciousness.[7]

The French physician Alfred Tomatis tells a story of the healing power of sound that took place at a Benedictine monastery in the South of France in the 1960s. Many of the monks fell ill, and the local doctors could not diagnose the cause. Tomatis was called in and after examining the monks and taking their personal histories, Tomatis believed he had discovered the source of the problem. Normally, the monks sang Gregorian Chants for six to eight hours a day. In the wake of church reforms, the new abbot decided that the monks should stop singing and do more practical tasks. Tomatis suggested the monks recommence their chanting. Within five months, each had restored his health.[8]

Sacred sound helps us connect our body and our soul, the most authentic aspect of ourselves which resides in our heart. We each have our own sound, our own resonance, and when we are in tune with our sacred sound, we are healthy and well. When we are out of tune, we are more susceptible to illness or stress.[9]

One of my favourite meditation practices is chanting mantras. Mantra is a Sanskrit term meaning "sacred speech." Mantras have been chanted for thousands of years. Traditionally, they were given by enlightened teachers, buddhas, and masters to students to help them realise their Divine essence. Wise spirit teachers tell us that mantras work beyond space and time. When we chant a mantra, we link with the energy that has been generated each time this mantra has been sung in any part of the world at any time—past, present, and future.

Mantras are important for three main reasons. First, they stimulate our energy system by invoking different higher vibrational energies that activate qualities of the awakened mind (such as unconditional love, compassion, joy, and wisdom). Regular mantra practice helps anchor these enlightened qualities within us. During the chanting, as we focus on the words, the mind quiets. After chanting and raising the energy, it is helpful to meditate for twenty-one minutes, bathing in the silence. This allows the light invoked to expand within and flow into every part of our being. The wave of energy grows, lifting us into a higher vibrational state and opening the door to the authentic Self.

Second, mantras are like liquid fire burning away and loosening the conditioning. As we chant and then sit in meditation, the conditioning can bubble up and we may experience some emotional and physical pain. In that moment, we can breathe with the rising sensations and let the energy pass through us and release from our body.

Third, chanting helps to open and clear our throat centre. This is an important centre of communication that may have been closed through the socialisation process.

Exercise 7. Who Am I?

To help you communicate with and expand your perspective of your authentic Self.

1. Sit quietly for a few minutes.

2. Bring your awareness to your breath. Take a deep breath in, and slowly let the breath out. Repeat three times. Allow your breathing to return to normal.

3. On your next inhale, imagine breathing into your heart and opening your heart centre. As you breathe out, imagine that the love you are flows from your heart into every cell of your body, filling every part of your being with light. Repeat four times, allowing the feelings of love and light to expand within you.

4.	Ask, "Who am I?" Look inwards. Wait and see what answer comes, if any. Are you the person you see in the mirror? Are you the body you inhabit? Who is asking the question? (If you hear nothing now, an answer may come later as a thought or in a dream.)

5.	After a while, gently bring yourself back by becoming conscious of your surroundings and when you are ready, open your eyes.

Keep asking the question. Allow your heart to speak to you in its own way and in its own time.

Chapter 17

Clearing a Path to the Awakened State

Meditation is the only way you can grow.
There's no other way out. Because when you
meditate you are in silence, you are in
thoughtless awareness. Then the growth of
awareness takes place.[1] —Shri Mataji
Nirmala Devi, Indian spiritual teacher

It is Sunday morning, the third day of my second meditation retreat. I'm restless. My mind hasn't settled. I'm filled with doubt. "I can't do this, meditation is pointless, I'm useless at it, my mind should be quiet by now, I'm doing it wrong." I start to question why I'm here. "I should give up meditating." Suddenly, everything changes, and I am enveloped in golden light. All thoughts disappear, and I bask in light, silence, love, and euphoria. Then, just as unexpectedly, the light vanishes, and the facilitator is bringing us back from the meditation. I have no idea what transpired and for how long. I only know I feel joyful, and I can't stop smiling. At breakfast, someone notices the change in me and asks what happened. I share my experience with the group, and the facilitator says, "You touched your essential nature, your inner light." I am so happy. I know I have to keep meditating.

What is Meditation?

Meditation is a spiritual practice of seated, focussed awareness. Ancient cultures across the globe created meditation practices to harness the power of the Divine inside the body and the universal life force energy (prana, in Sanskrit, and chi, in Chinese). These practices were designed to unite the body and mind, awaken the Divine heart and evolve the non dualism of mind. Meditation, in this context, is a way of rediscovering the truth of who we are, of building a bridge to our authentic Self.

Meditation is not about acquiring peace of mind; that is a by-product. Meditation is a tool for personal growth—to gain insight and clarity, and develop awareness and authentic power. In the silence of the meditation space, we intend to become the observer, the one who is aware of all that is happening in the continually unfolding now. We learn to detach, to listen, and to act in alignment with the flow of life, the universal power of Divine order.

In meditation, as beginners and at the beginning of each meditation practice, we are growing the life force energy, or prana, within ourselves. As the energy increases, our consciousness expands and we can experience the world and ourselves from a more encompassing perspective. We may realise that there is more to life than our everyday existence.

Through regular practice, our consciousness can develop to such a degree that we transform our physical reality. Our body, speech, and mind become the body, speech, and mind of the Divine Self.

Why Is Meditation Essential?

In the quiet space of meditation, we can hear the voice of our soul and become aware of our Divine light. We meditate to find the place within ourselves where the ego mind ceases and the voice of the wise Self, can be heard. The mind disconnects us from our true Self, and meditation helps to overcome this. In essence, meditation helps us prevail over the inherent grasping quality of the mind, so that we can experience the grace of the connection with our Divine essence and clear the path to the awakened state.

*Meditation is essential because it can
transcend the mind to experience silence.*

During meditation, it is important to stay as accepting and respectful as we can with whatever is happening within us (especially with the mind), moment to moment. Whilst we meditate, we will have thoughts. It is impossible not to have thoughts, until we reach the enlightened state as I found out through the coma experience.

When you become aware that you are immersed in thoughts, detach from them without criticism. Say to the mind with compassion, "Come back and listen to the silence." Refocus in your heart centre and the mind quietens until the next thought arises. When the silence comes, say, "This is a good thing." Even if the mind wanders throughout the meditation and you keep bringing your focus inside, that is fine. You are learning to tame the mind.

The gap between thoughts is the space of awareness. This space can grow the more we practice. Eventually, our mind may stay silent throughout most of the meditation. Our job in meditation is to favour the present moment and the silence within, over any thoughts that arise.

Experiencing periods of stillness—even for a few seconds—is a gift of meditation. When we keep returning to the silence, the connection to the authentic Self opens and some insight may arise. This is the awakened state speaking to us, giving us a taste of what it is like and to recognise its voice. In one practice, I felt the biblical verse "the truth shall make you free" (John 8:32 KJV) in every cell of my body and I knew it to be true. When insights like this happen we carry the understanding within us, in our body. The inner wisdom becomes an embodied experience, a cell memory, and the insight is realised in our life. This is how we embody our awakening.

This connection to the authentic Self is crucial. Once this connection has opened, it can reopen. But when we become anxious or judgemental and mistrust the process, the connection can also close.

Through our continued practice, the inner connection strengthens and we recognise the different state. Things that used to irritate us become meaningless, and are replaced by more important issues, such as our life path. As a result, we may find ourselves making changes in our external world that align us with our new inner awareness. Perhaps we watch less television, eat more healthily, and associate with people who are also on a spiritual path.

Further Benefits of Meditation

Meditation also offers you many emotional, physical, mental and spiritual gifts.

Present moment awareness. You can only be aware in the present, not in the future or the past. In meditation, you focus in the present as the observer. The unfolding potential of the present is the place of spiritual growth, and the domain of the authentic Self.

Improved health. An increasing body of scientific research is proving what the ancients and meditators have long known: meditation can change your body and mind in positive ways through nurturing qualities such as altruism, equanimity, love, and compassion. It can rewire your neural circuitry making it easier to change your harmful habits.[2] At a physical level, meditation may also boost your immune system[3] and reduce the need for painkillers.[4]

Deep relaxation. Meditation significantly lowers brain wave frequency. At the beginning of your practice your brain moves from the gamma and beta waves of higher mental activity and active thinking into the alpha waves of relaxation. As you continue meditating you experience the theta waves of deep relaxation.[5] Occasionally your brain may even shift into the delta waves associated with dreamless sleep. Whilst in the delta state you may have no conscious recollection of your meditation practice. According to Nepalese shaman, Bhola, Nath Banstola, this is when profound healing takes place.[6]

Inner voice awareness. During the theta brainwave state you access your intuition. Some arising perceptions make so much sense you may wonder why you never thought of them before. Others may bump against your comfort zone and actioning them is challenging. For example, prior to my first monthly team meeting as the new coordinator in a stress management project, I thought to end the meeting with a meditation and a safe sharing space. When the notion first appeared to me in a meditation, I dismissed it immediately. Then it emerged again and again. Finally, despite trepidation, I introduced the idea and for three years, we held this sharing space. It brought us closer as a work team and as friends.

How many times have you disregarded your inner voice and then regretted it? According to Elisabeth Haich, the late Hungarian spiritual teacher, the challenge is to value the inner voice and action what it says. Many hear it, but few attend to it.[7]

Quieter mind. First, the action of continually bringing your focus back from your thoughts to your heart centre is a valuable way to quiet the mind. Second, when you consciously take deep inhales and slow exhales, you activate the parasympathetic nervous system (PNS). The PNS is a key component in helping people stay calm and focussed even when faced with upsetting memories or situations.[8] Suggestion: Use both of these techniques in your everyday life, especially when you are feeling anxious. And, in meditation stay focussed on the whole of the out breath, and then pause before inhaling.

Greater self-acceptance. Meditation invites you to meet yourself in all your various moods and mind-sets. You gradually learn to relax and accept whatever arises. In doing so you accept yourself, and realise nothing needs to be resisted, denied, or suppressed. You can allow each emerging sensation to move through you and be released. In this way, meditation also teaches you to remain steady, in flow with life.

Heavy energy clearance. During meditation when high vibrational energy (HVE) moves through the body, you may experience physical pain as the HVE dissolves blocks in your meridian energy channels. If this happens, breathe into the discomfort to aid the clearing.

Life review. Whilst meditating, memories may surface. As the memory unfolds, ask, "What are you teaching me? What is releasing?" Meditation is a safe space for you to reconcile past incidents. This may feel like a gentle life review that some people describe during a near-death experience. It is a reminder that everything counts. In the awakening process, our karma has to be purified.

Five Suggestions to Sustain a Meditation Practice

During meditation, you may become deterred by your wandering mind. This is common. Here are five suggestions to help facilitate a regular, daily, seated meditation practice.

1. Designate an area in your home for meditation.
2. Set a regular time each day to meditate.
3. Practice with a local meditation group.
4. Explore different techniques (for example, watch the breath, walk while feeling every part of the movement, feel gratitude, or extend healing thoughts to others).
5. Reflect on the ways the practice is helping you.

Exercise 8. A Practice of Unconditional Love

This practice to access the power of unconditional love within is based on a meditation in Fotoula Adrimi's book The Golden

Book of Wisdom: Ancient Spirituality and Shamanism for Modern Times.[9]

1. Sit quietly for a few minutes, focussing on your breaths in and out, intending to relax and quiet your mind. Imagine that you are breathing in love from the world, and breathing out your love to the world. With each breath, intend to open your heart centre until your inner radiance shines out.

2. Say three times, "I am the love of the world."

3. Allow the power of love to flow from your heart into your body. Let love flow to all your tissues and organs and into every part of you. Ask the power of love, "Please heal, reveal, and embrace all aspects of my being." Meditate for five minutes.

4. In this space of inner radiance, let love flow from your heart to all beings, to the planet, to all the places in the world, to the rich and poor, the cities and mountains, the schools and war zones. Do this without judgement, resentment, and anger. Let the love flow to all the governments, corporations, and other institutions and their employees without prejudice. Divine love is there for all, no matter what they have done and who they are.

5. Say three times, "I am the power of love."

6. Meditate for ten minutes, radiating the power of love to all.

7. Focus in your heart centre, which is glowing like a star. Give thanks to yourself for creating a positive shift in your life and the world reality. Say, "May this state of unconditional love become my cell memory."

8. Gently bring your awareness back out into the room and open your eyes.

#

Throughout your life you have built relationships with family, friends, partners, animals, and the Earth. You have given yourself to the external world. Meditation asks you to bring your awareness inside, build a relationship with yourself, and reconnect with your inner light.

The interplay between inward focus and outward attention is a continual movement of energy. The more you keep your focus inside, the weaker the attachments to the outside become. Consequently, the easier it will be to remain steady and centred in your own Self no matter what is happening externally.

Chapter 18

Healing Deeply and Elevating Consciousness

I am lying in a small, circular glass cabin with a turf roof, surrounded by trees. I am nervous and excited. I have no idea what is about to happen. The shamanic practitioner Two Birds is drumming. "Are you ready to receive your soul parts back into your body?" she asks. "Yes," I say. At some point, I am aware that the drumming has stopped and Two Birds is blowing something into my chest and rattling around my body, sealing the healing. Slowly, I become more conscious of my surroundings. Two Birds explains what has taken place: negative energy was extracted and lost soul parts were returned. This is the first of many soul retrievals that I will experience over the coming years. I know all these soul parts are returning to help me become whole. I am grateful to all the healers and all the soul parts that have come back.

Soul Loss and Trauma

I first read about the concept of soul retrieval in Sandra Ingerman's book *Soul Retrieval: Mending the Fragmented Self*,[1] and knew instantly that it would help me in my healing journey. Indigenous shamans from North and South America and the Himalayas believe that when we experience a traumatic event, a part of our soul can be too frightened to remain in the situation. The soul part leaves our body and goes into a spirit realm. Any event, from a minor accident such as a fall from a bike to a violent assault, has the potential to create soul loss—depending on our reaction. A situation that triggers soul loss in one person may not impact another.

During a traumatic event, some people may be consciously aware of leaving their body, dissociating, and watching from above as the event unfolds. In her book *Unbroken*,[2] Madeleine Black describes alternating between watching herself from above being raped, and being back in her body and experiencing the assault.

When the event ends, the dissociated soul part may return to the body or it may be too traumatised and remain outside the body in another dimension, suspended in time, until it is either brought back by a healer or returns through our spiritual or personal work. It is also common for traumatic events to result in memory loss. If the person is too shocked during the event, the soul part that leaves may be the only part that is aware of what happened. The person may not recall anything until, years later, something triggers an awareness. In Madeleine's case, her daughter turning thirteen triggered memories and flashbacks of her rape at that age.

As a therapist, I have supported several people who have spoken about this. They were not coping well in life, but did not understand why. They had no conscious memory of being raped, sexually abused, or something equally traumatic until years later when something prompted their memory, such as a particular smell or the sound of a door closing. In his book, *The Body Keeps the Score*, Bessel van der Kolk, the Dutch psychiatrist, author, and educator, states, "Traumatic memories are precipitated by specific triggers. When one element of a traumatic experience is triggered, other elements are likely to automatically flow."[3]

Even if we know what happened, we can still experience soul loss if something mentally or emotionally disturbs us. This can be true of all the shocking events in our life: abuse, an accident, the death of a loved one, or a job loss. Soul loss can happen in circumstances that might appear trivial to others: being shouted at by a parent or teacher, bullied by a peer, or startled by a well-meaning family member or colleague.

According to Ingerman, soul loss is not an uncommon phenomenon and it can happen multiple times and at any stage in our life. Soul loss and traumatic experiences may cause some people to function automatically, without thought or emotion, in order to cope with their day-to-day life. In the West, we have had no frame of reference for soul loss. Perhaps this is the aspect that dissociation misses. As more Westerners train as shamanic practitioners and healers, these ancient understandings and healing methods are becoming more widely known.

If we are fragmented and soul parts are missing, then it is not possible to awaken fully in a grounded way. The lost soul parts will continue to impact us and we will keep relying on behaviours that we unconsciously instigated to compensate for the loss and cope.

Soul Retrieval

As with all personal work, the return of lost soul parts can only be done in stages to allow time for each returned part to integrate into our body and psyche. We also have to nurture the part that has come back, and the shamanic practitioner may offer some guidance about what a returned soul part needs to assimilate. Although some soul parts cannot return without a form of soul retrieval intervention by an experienced healer, other parts may come back spontaneously through either insights from our personal and spiritual work or by overcoming limiting behaviour patterns.

In 2019, I was spending a week at a bothy (one-bedroom hut) in Glen Lyon, Scotland. In the mountains above where I was staying is a well-known horseshoe of four munros (mountains over three thousand feet). At the start of my holiday, I had no intention of climbing the munros. On my next to last day while out walking, I found myself on the path to the first munro Càrn Gorm. I climbed the smaller hill in front of the munro and thought, "I could climb the munro." Next morning, I knew I had to. I climbed three of the four munros before my body and mind said "enough," and I headed back to the bothy. I felt elated. I was amazed that my body had coped with the physical exertion. Something in me had shifted.

A few days later, I realised that I had had a spontaneous soul retrieval. The last time I had put my body through this level of exertion was in 2009, hill walking in Peru, where I experienced altitude sickness and eventually ended up in a coma. Unconsciously, the experience had left me fearful of stressing my body, and in the process, I had stopped hill walking altogether. That day in Scotland, I reclaimed the soul part that enjoyed the adventure of hill walking and being in nature. I felt energised and alive and resumed hill walking.

Other Lives—Healing the Past

Through my healing journey, I have seen how some of my missing soul parts had been stranded in time, lost in other lifetimes.

As part of my spiritual practice I have worked with the Rays of Divine Consciousness. The Rays, and their associated meditation practices, are a profound way of working with high vibrational energies. At the same time, they have shown me where I hold negative karma and separation patterns, which manifest as blocked energy in my body. In seeking help to clear some of these blocks, I have gone to Fotoula Adrimi for ISIS Energy Healing.

Often, as I have lain on the healing table, Fotoula has gently guided me into a past life regression, and images and feelings come to me of myself in other experiences and in other lives. Some visions are powerful and even excruciatingly painful. The pain eventually dissipates as Fotoula continues to channel the energy into my body and walk me through the vision. Thankfully, most times, all I see in my mind's eye are the general circumstances of what is taking place. During the regression, unskillful acts, either my or others', are atoned for through compassion and forgiveness, and the respective soul parts still trapped in the experience are released.

Sometimes, the regressions show unresolved issues that my soul is here to work through in my current life.

Some readers may find the idea of past lives strange or far-fetched. I do not know whether these lives actually happened or not. When I am in the regressions, my physical and emotional responses are so real that I do not doubt them. Through the process, I have learned that I do not need to know if they are real or imagined. I have faith that something outside my conscious awareness is being addressed. The proof is the absence of the energy block, and the renewed lightness and well-being I feel at the end of the session.

On Pilgrimage

"We leave something of ourselves behind when we leave a place; we stay there, even though we go away. And there are things in us that we can find again only by going back there,"[4] writes Pascal Mercier (aka Peter Bieri).

Many spiritual teachers, such as the Dalai Lama, advocate the benefit of pilgrimages and travels to other lands. It opens our awareness to other people, different cultures, and alternative ways of living. Pilgrimages to sacred sites, such as temples and stone circles, around the world can offer us healing opportunities as we experience the high vibrational energies anchored there by spiritual people long ago. Pilgrimages may also be a way of reconnecting with parts of ourselves from other lives. Sometimes we may feel drawn to visit a particular place, unaware that it may be part of our healing journey and that a hidden gift our soul carries can be activated.

Over the years, I have visited many sacred sites around the world and experienced remarkable gifts and healings. My first déjà vu happened on a visit to Egypt in 2010. As I walked around the Meidum Pyramid, I suddenly adopted a completely different gait, my head was bowed in reverence, and in my mind's eye, I saw myself as a man dressed in a robe with a cloth draped over my left arm. I could feel the sanctity of the land. Due to the presence of police inspectors, our group could only spend ten minutes inside the pyramid. I recall my reluctance to leave as our guide dragged me back to the minibus.

In March 2011, a group of us returned to Egypt and visited the Meidum Pyramid. Inside, we spontaneously began chanting the gayatri mantra—one of the oldest and most powerful mantras from the Rig Veda (sacred Hindu texts). The mantra invokes the light of creation to dispel ego mind-sets. As I chanted, something in my throat centre opened, and a powerful deep voice emerged. I was stunned. The next day, we visited the Red Pyramid at Dashur, and again, chanted the gayatri mantra. In the pyramid's inner chamber, the power came into my voice again. For two hours, until the pyramid closed, we sang the mantra. I felt joyous. My throat centre, the seat of expression and communication, which had been shut down through various childhood experiences, has remained open, and my voice has become a powerful healing tool. In my energy healing sessions with clients, I find myself toning and chanting instinctively. I had reclaimed this gift that had lain dormant within me, and I needed to go to Egypt to do it.

The Tipping Point—A Shift in Consciousness

During my 2008 visit (chapter 9), Emaho took a group of us to dinner at his favourite restaurant. I was seated next to

Emaho something I had not consciously chosen as I was still nervous in his presence. On his website, Emaho lists recommended films, and at some point, he turned to me and said, "I think I'll put short descriptions under each film about what to look for." I immediately replied that it was a great idea. He looked at me, but said nothing more. The weeks past and no descriptions appeared on his website. I eventually understood something about myself. I had reacted to Emaho's suggestion from the part of me that needed someone to "tell me what to look for. Tell me how I should feel when I watch the film or what scene I should focus on. Tell me what to do. Fix my problems. Fix my life." I was looking to Emaho for answers instead of trusting myself. I laughed as I recalled the many times I had checked the website and stared dumbfounded that there was still nothing written about the films.

Since then, I have continued to do my spiritual practice and work through the initiations that life brings. Then, one day, I sensed a change. I knew I had crossed the tipping point, and that, due to all the inner work, my authentic Self was now stronger than the egoic self. The balance had shifted within me to the wise Self. The tail was no longer wagging the dog.

This shift happens for us all at some point. Intuitively, you know you have reached your tipping point when your authentic Self is stronger. I have faith that when enough of us raise our consciousness, the collective consciousness will also reach a tipping point. The higher states of awareness that many of us are experiencing individually create ripple effects out into the world that everyone can benefit from. Wise spirit teachers have said that the influence of people who reach elevated states of cognizance is far greater than those who resonate at lower vibrations.

An awakened individual has an
immense positive impact globally.

In *Power vs. Force*,[5] David R. Hawkins demonstrates how each person who has attained the higher states of consciousness of love, joy, and peace can counterbalance thousands of individuals with lower levels of awareness.

A few weeks after I woke up from the coma and still experiencing an expanded state of consciousness, I was supervising a group of counsellors at a centre in Glasgow. We were allocated a different room, smaller than our normal space. The group that day shared honestly and deeply. At the end of the session, two participating counsellors told me that it was the most heartfelt and powerful group they had experienced. "Was it the smaller room?" one asked. "Maybe," I said. Instinctively, I knew it had been because of my post-coma elevated state of consciousness. That day, we all experienced a gift of the living light that was coming through me, and that was bringing more awareness.

Chapter 19

Receiving Help from the Spirit Realms

Our spirit guides are universal forces that are
here to help us.[1] —Aletheia Luna, spiritual writer

I have just told the person I love that I cannot be with her.
I have made a commitment to follow my heart, and it is
taking me in a different direction. The irony is not lost on
either of us. We are both devastated. I go to bed, but cannot
sleep. My mind and emotions are in turmoil. It is painful
to hurt someone I love. At midnight, I step outside. Looking
up at the sky, I am about to ask, "Am I doing the right
thing?" when I see an enormous shooting star. I take this
as a sign. I drop to my knees. Life has been watching me
and responded, confirming my decision. Tears of gratitude
flow. In the days and weeks to come, as my partner and I
slowly separate, the memory of this astral corroboration
helps me stay strong.

Building a Relationship with Our Spirit Guides

In the months following my first experience of awakening in 1995, precipitated by an inner desire to discover what was happening to me, I regularly visited new age shops. As I entered each shop, either Native American (NA) music would be playing or start playing. The hairs on the back of my neck would rise, and I had the distinct sense that the music was telling me something, although I had no idea what. Then, suddenly everything NA fascinated me. I found myself buying NA jewellery, and twice, I went to hear a Maori woman channel an NA spirit guide. Yet, channelling was then so incompatible with my level of understanding and comfort zone that I never went back.

At the time, I had no one to ask what these occurrences meant and the experiences stopped. Then in 2007, odd things began happening again. First, was the shooting star I described above. After that, library books would literally fall off the shelf in front of me. Every book was about how spirit helpers communicate with people and written by people who spoke with the spirit world, such as William Bloom's *Working With Angels, Fairies, and Nature Spirits.*[2]

I read the books and started to feel what I now know are spirit beings touching the right side of my head. I could feel their presence around me, even though I could not see anything. The books opened a door of understanding. Now I could relate my experiences to what I was reading. Spirit guides were making themselves known to me. They come to us usually on the right side—but I had no idea why or what they were saying.

Out of the blue, I found the business card of the woman with whom I had done an introductory personal development course six years previously. I phoned Christine to ask if she was still doing the next level of the course, the weeklong Avatar workshop. She said she had not taught the course for several years, but had recently picked up the material again and we agreed to do the course one-on-one. During an exercise at the end of the week, we sat facing each other. Looking into each other's eyes, I could feel my whole face physically change—as if I was becoming someone else. From Christine's expression, I knew she could see the change that I felt. Afterwards, she told me my face completely changed into the face of an NA man. At another workshop, two years later, the same thing happened to me.

I later discovered that this is a process known as "transfiguration," where others witness the spirit beings who come through our body. I now know that the NA man who showed on my face is one of my main healing guides. People who follow a spiritual and healing path often have a team of helpers from the spirit realms who support them with their soul development and healing work.

Now, in my energy healing work with clients, I am accustomed to my spirit guides coming through my body and directing the healing session, or using my voice to chant and tone sounds that augment the energy being channelled. In my counselling sessions, I often see little starbursts of light behind clients. From experience, I understand that these are beings of light letting me know they are present and supporting the client, myself, and the healing work that is being done in the session. These spirit beings, who can be the client's or my helpers, are like the imaginary friends some of us had in childhood.

Like the siddhis (spiritual gifts), having spirit helpers can be part of our development process. These helpers will make contact with us in various ways. Stay open in the process and pay attention to coincidences, synchronicities, and other unusual phenomena. If you feel spirit beings are trying to attract your attention, you may wish to read books about connecting with spirit guides to gain more knowledge. You could also contact a psychic medium to guide your process, communicate with the beings, and suggest what to do and how to set boundaries.

The important thing is to develop a good relationship with your spirit helpers and to only ally with those who work fully and wholly for the Light, those whose sole intention is to support your highest good. Else, these beings can be detrimental to our personal growth and spiritual development. If you are unsure, ask your spirit guides to step back. You are in charge. Also, if they see you are uncomfortable, they might step away until another time, as my own guides did after the channelling event.

Exercise 9. Making Contact with Your Spirit Guides

To invite your spirit helpers to support you.

1. Bring your focus inside your body. For a few minutes imagine breathing into your heart and breathing out from your heart.

2. Invite your spirit guides of the light to come close to you and create a sacred, protected space around you.

3. Ask your main spirit helper to make their presence known to you in some way. Say that you wish to

ask for their support. Wait to see what happens. You can ask questions, such as, "Who are you?" "How can I work with you?"

4.   Gently, bring your focus back into the room.

5.   Thank your spirit guides of the light. Close the sacred space by asking the guides to make sure that you and your space are completely sealed and protected before they leave.

When you invoke these beings of light, they come close to your aura, which raises your vibration. In this space of heightened awareness you may feel, see or hear your spirit helpers. As you practice connecting with them a supportive relationship may develop. These beings have no personal agenda. They only wish to support your soul development.

The Earth—A School for Soul Evolution

The beings of light wish to share their perspective of the Earth. According to these wise teachers, souls come to Earth to learn lessons, purify their karma from this and other lifetimes, become aware of who they are whilst living in a body, and raise their vibration. The Earth School is all about: embodying our higher, divine, conscious-ness.

These beings of light add that, when we die, we return to the spirit realms where, free from the conditioned physical body, we are able to embrace a wider perspective to human life. There are opportunities in the spirit realms and back in the material world for souls to continue their journey.

Most souls who transition (die) do not want to move on right away. They wish to stay around the Earth and wait for family and friends. In the meantime, their guides may take them to places where they can observe people doing spiritual practices, meditating, or holding a ceremony. Testing their readiness to advance, their guides may ask, "What did you see?" The soul's development continues whether they are in a physical body or not.

Some souls who do move on wish to return to Earth shortly after their physical death and try again. Maybe the soul will make different choices or maybe it will again become discouraged from spiritual development by old tapes. Doors keep opening for the soul to live its life's purpose, but the choice is up to the soul. A soul may live the same life many times until it learns a particular lesson. Alternatively, some souls who do move on decide to stay longer in the spirit realms before reincarnating.

Once a soul has moved to a higher vibration, the beings of light say to it, "OK, in your level of frequency, you have these soul lessons to access that are particular to you." The soul's guides and the soul then make a plan for the next incarnation, and in this way, the process of soul growth continues. We may wonder how many lifetimes we have lived. The answer, say the beings of light, is unimportant. It does not matter how many lifetimes. We cannot remember them and yet everything is planned and recorded.

Our higher Self—our spirit, the aspect of ourselves that does not incarnate—keeps a record of everything we experience, every thought we have, everything we have ever done here on Earth. Yet, this record has little value while we are on Earth. The vibration we grow into whilst we are alive has value and is worthy of our focus. At some point, as our spiritual practice continues, our vibration increases. And the energy waves that we emit resonate with the energy waves of the enlightened state. Then, we will be completely free of the earthly illusion.

Exercise 10. Working with the Light of Your Divine Heart

To radiate the light of your soul. (A practice from the spirit guides of the light.)

1. Before going to sleep each night, say, "Like the moon, I radiate the light of One," three times.

2. When you awake, say, "I am the brilliant sun radiating light in the infinite space," three times.

The guides say that when you do this exercise you allow the light of your soul to radiate throughout the night and day, no matter if you are aware of it or not. This is a way for you to support yourself and all beings.

PART V

LIGHTING THE PATH: THE HEART

Chapter 20

Embracing the Heart Wave

[I]t's being willing ... to take risks, that changes us.
It grows us. It matures us. We find out who we
are by taking risks.[1] —Meredith Little Foster

A collective wave of energy has been weaving a path around the Earth for some time and gathering momentum. Some people were born surfing this wave, what I call the "heart wave." Others are either unaware of its presence or have no urge to catch it.

In 2007, at age fifty, I stepped fully onto the heart wave and what a ride it has been. Some experiences have been wild, unnerving, miraculous, and nothing my mind could have envisioned. The heart wave has carried me through the highs and lows of its tumultuous waters, increasing its power and momentum the longer I remain. At times, the wave has dumped me into the deep sea, before picking me up and carrying me to a safe haven. It has continuously challenged me to swim with its currents and remain steady in its surges. It has promised me nothing, and yet offers me everything.

When I find myself beached and breathless, I get back on it in trust.

I do not know where this wave is carrying me. I only know choosing to get on it has been the best thing I ever did. One of the beautiful things about the heart wave is that it is universal and personal. All can ride the heart wave, yet everyone's experience of the wave will be unique. The heart wave carries each of us to all the places we need to go both within and outside of ourselves. It helps us encounter the people and situations we need to meet to resolve the karma our soul is carrying.

This wave has never lied to me or overwhelmed me, even as I neared its edge. It is not interested in my comfort—only in my highest good. This wave is alive in me. I am the heart wave.

The Sacred Heart

In the same way that our mind has been compromised by the conditioning, our heart has been similarly undermined. When we talk about the heart, we need to differentiate between the emotional, conditioned heart and the sacred, Divine heart within us.

In this book, when I speak about the heart, I am referring to the sacred heart. The ancient Egyptian spiritual teachings on life and death describe the sacred heart as wise, knowledgeable, observant and aware of all that we do, skilful and unskilful.[2] The sacred heart is the enlightened state, the soul, the Divine spark within.

Unskilful actions weigh heavily on our sacred heart, and consciously or unconsciously, we carry this weight inside.

Other traditions may say we carry "heavy karma." Whether we are aware or unaware of this weight during our life, at death, we have the opportunity to acknowledge it. That is why the ancient teachings recommended that people live life in accordance with Divine justice, respectful of all life. Both in life and death, a light heart, free from the weight of karma, holds the key to inner happiness and joy.

The sacred heart is an expression of unconditional love and wisdom, and is unaffected by all that happens to us during our life. The sacred heart knows that in this experience of life, we are educating our ego mind to see and trust the heart's purity, expansiveness, wholeness, and Divine nature. It knows that on Earth the soul's lesson is all about love.

Perseverance and Courage

> When you get into a tight place, and everything goes against you till it seems as if you couldn't hold on a minute longer, *never give up then*, for that's just the place and time that the tide'll turn.[3]
> —Harriet Beecher Stowe, American abolitionist and author

Change involves breaking habits. And breaking habits takes time. It takes time to recognise the unhelpful patterns we carry, and it requires many small steps to try out new choices. To succeed, we persevere in the process, especially when we slip up. Even though the mind has perpetuated the same behaviour for years, it can get disgruntled when change is not immediate. In this journey, we are asked to develop trust and exercise patience.

Change also necessitates courage. It takes courage to overcome the voice of the risk averse mind and walk away from the subscribed path. We are leaving people and situations that no longer support our inner growth. We are ceasing to collude with others in mutual, self-sabotage. We are refraining from being the people pleaser, the fixer, the rescuer, the victim or the perpetrator, or any other well-worn role. Courage raises us to a higher level of consciousness that makes positive change possible. Ironically, when we make the choices that are right for us, we often do not feel courageous. We are simply doing what we know we need to do. "What a relief," says our inner voice, "At last."

In 2018, at a writers' festival in Stirling, Scotland, Louise Penny, an internationally acclaimed author, spoke about giving up her career for her dream to write a book. Her husband offered to support her, and then for five years, she experienced writer's block. Fear stopped her writing. Finally, one day, she gave herself permission to write anything, and that started the creative process that led to her first book.

Giving yourself permission to just put pen to paper, make a mistake, and try without attachment to an outcome are expressions of courage that can propel you out of the inertia of fearful thinking into creative action and a new life. What would you like to give yourself permission to do?

Honesty and Sincerity

Honesty is another key for transformation. Truth dissolves the lies of the mind. Seeing clearly strengthens us. The heart's path asks us to stop lying to ourselves. We stop pretending to be right when we know we have made a mistake. We stop defending the facade, the illusory self, and allow the light, vulnerability, and power of our authentic Self to be unmasked.

Just as honesty with ourselves is vital for happiness, so is a sincere wish for inner change. When your efforts are sincere, life hears you. The outcome may not be what you expect or come when you want it, but your sincerity will be answered. Life listens to your sacred heart. Enquire: "What do I wish to change?" "Who would I be without this impediment?"

Expansion and Contraction

Through personal work and spiritual practices, particularly ceremonies and rituals, we can move into expanded states of consciousness. Moments of clarity and infinite grace can open up as we touch the light of our Divine Self. This may last a few minutes, a few hours, or even days, but will eventually subside.

In 2018, I supported my friend Claudia Wolff birth her first moondance circle in Germany. During and after the ceremony, I was in a heightened state of consciousness. I felt joyful. Then, after a week, I noticed that I did not feel quite as happy and was getting upset by old issues (such as money concerns) and feeling exposed (by writing this book). The expanded state had loosened another layer of shadow, which had contracted my earlier feelings of expansion. After sessions with my counsellor and energy healer, together with my regular spiritual practices, I was able to release the energy of the old stories that had surfaced and happiness returned.

Contractions invariably follow expansions in personal growth, and generally, the bigger the expansion, the greater the contraction. Are you really taking two steps forward and three steps back? No, but it may feel that way sometimes, because personal growth is not linear. It is a continual process of unfolding and integration that allows you to rebalance your spiritual, mental, and emotional systems and anchor the openings and expansions into your body. This helps you consolidate your inner foundation in time for the next period of growth. Expansions and contractions are part of the cycle of growth.

If you experience a period of expansion and then things appear to be going awry, it may be a natural period of contraction as you rebalance. The higher state of consciousness may also be loosening more of your shadow, showing you what you need to heal and release so that you can return to the higher state. Rather than be dismayed by the apparent loss of progress and downturn in your mood, you can view each contraction as evidence of growth. Adopting an even bigger perspective, you may be healing years of inner separation—your own as well as from inherited family and ancestral patterns.

Unconditional Love—The Highest Power Available to Us

Seated in meditation, I suddenly feel an opening in my heart centre. Images of friends, one after another, appear in my mind's eye, and love flows spontaneously from my heart to each of them. Pictures of politicians appear, and still, love and compassion flow from my heart. There is no judgement and no change in the outpouring of love. I see people whom I have had difficulty with during my life and love continues to flow.

Spirituality is a quest towards opening the sacred, Divine heart. The earthly challenge is to embrace and embody unconditional love, a power that has no expectations. This power says to each of us that no matter who we are and no matter what we have done, I offer you the gift of unconditional love. Unconditional love is not expressed through the mind or through the emotions, but through our spirit. It is the pure love of spirit. When we walk a spiritual path, it is this love that we are called to personify.

Unconditional love is an openness of the heart that we may be able to feel through spiritual practice and connection with our soul. Unconditional love accepts us fully and invites us to fully accept ourselves and the world as it is.

Even though we may not understand what that means at this moment, it is possible to find complete love—not through a partner or a child or a pet, but within ourselves through union with our Divine heart. Our challenge on Earth is to wholly embrace this power that the hurt part of us shields. This Divine union is the fourth facet of awakening.

What Would Love Do?

When we are faced with a dilemma, our natural reaction can be to think our way out of the situation. Instead of using the mind to resolve a predicament, we can sit quietly and ask, "What would love do?"

With permission, I share my friend Eddie's story (not his real name). Eddie phoned me for guidance on a delicate family matter. He had a one-night stand and impregnated the woman. The woman wanted to keep the child, and Eddie's immediate reaction was for her to abort. I asked Eddie to take some time by himself, to quiet his mind, to connect with his heart, and ask, "What would love do?" Eddie called me a few days later. His heart had made a choice and he had decided to accept its advice. He had spoken to the woman and said that if she wanted to keep the child, he would support her choice. Eddie also told me that his mother had experienced a similar situation, although in her case, the father refused to accept his child—him. Now the familial pattern was ending with Eddie's decision to acknowledge and support the woman and their unborn child.

When I ask myself "What would love do?" I am often in awe at how quickly an answer comes. When I follow through with the guidance, issues can resolve quickly and in a way my mind would not have contemplated. Suggestion: Think of a situation in your life. If you ask, "What would love do?" what answer arises?

Unconditional love offers us a way to end the internal and external conflicts and replace the struggle with inner happiness, acceptance, and joy.

Chapter 21

Moving Away from Cause and Effect

True forgiveness and love arise naturally,
effortlessly, from the silence of the heart broken
all the way open,[1] —Gangaji, spiritual teacher
and author

Sitting in my hall again and connecting within, I can feel a large knot of energy in my solar plexus. I sense sadness and pain. Intuitively, I realise this has come from the judgements, anger, and accusations of others that I have absorbed through ignorance, guilt, and feelings of inadequacy. As I breathe into the knot, forgiveness spontaneously arises from my heart and surrounds the knot. The knot loosens. I see how I have taken on the abuse and pain that others have projected, and how I, too, have condemned myself and others. After an hour, the knot has eased but something still remains, showing me I have more work to do. How much forgiveness do I need to extend to myself? "Infinite forgiveness," says my wise Self.

Forgiveness Liberates—It Sets you Free

Wise teachers say that forgiveness does not mean that we turn the other cheek when someone is unkind, rude, or aggressive, and say, "It's OK. I forgive you." This only condones (and encourages) the other person's misbehaviour. To avoid conflict, we cede our personal power. That is not forgiveness.

Forgiveness is when we let go of what someone did to us. We release the burden of the energy of the abuse from our body. We let go of the weight of past events. For example, when I was twelve, a choir teacher made a derogatory remark about my singing. Years later, I found myself still thinking about that person and what he did, still blaming him for silencing me, and carrying the resentment. The realisation allowed me to forgive him and finally put the burden down. As I share in chapter 18, I have now rediscovered the gift of singing and the power of healing that comes from my voice.

True forgiveness is a kindness towards ourselves to let go of our millstones. However, it is not easy to practice. Forgiveness asks us to meet all aspects of ourselves with honesty, the shadow as well as the light.

Forgiving Ourselves

Can we really forgive ourselves? Can we really forgive others? The forgiveness we deny others is an aspect of the forgiveness we deny ourselves. If we can forgive ourselves unconditionally, we let go of the hurt and discover nothing remains to forgive in others.

When something happens to us, or when someone hurts us, a part of our mind can keep us attached to the hurt and stuck in victimhood, and the pain fossilizes our identity. Part of us stays frozen in time, unable to move on. We may keep reexperiencing the hurt without letting it go. If we do not do the personal work to release the pain, we can find ourselves going around in circles, facing the same issue over and over. Even with personal work, we may find that the issue resurfaces, showing us that another layer has to be released and healed until all that remains is our inner Light. We may also find that some of the pain is due to self-blame and shame for what happened.

The layers of hurt could be from disappointment, anger, resentment, and more. We may be too frightened and too bitter to let them go. Our attachment to these layers creates its own stories in our mind about past events and people— in other words, our version of reality. Keep shining the light on the layers of pain in order to transmute them, one by one, and uncover what lies beneath. When you do, you realise that the person needing your forgiveness most is yourself, and this may be the last person you offer it to unconditionally. Lasting peace is possible.

Exercise 11. Bring Forgiveness into Your Everyday Life

This is a two-stage practice of detachment and transformation to help you act from a place of forgiveness.

1. *Detach and Reflect.* When you get angry or upset with someone or a situation, pause and detach. Become the observer. Acknowledge and release the feelings, and reflect. Ask, "What do I need to say or do in this situation for my highest good?" The

intention is to take responsibility for your emotional reactions, and respond with clarity and compassion for the highest outcome for yourself and the other person. According to the late American psychologist and mediator Marshall Rosenberg, "What others do may be a stimulus of our feelings, but not the cause."[2]

Everything that happens in your life follows the universal law of cause and effect. When you detach from the situation and accept what happened without directing blame, you are able to access a place of no cause and effect. You put down the burden, and step into your authentic power.

2.   *Transform.* Once detached from the hurt, you can transform it into compassion and forgiveness. How? Imagine the other person in their Divine essence and release any judgement. You are transforming your reaction into awareness of the person's Divine light. Intend that compassion and forgiveness radiate out from your heart to yourself and the other person. This elevates the process from the human perspective to that of the eternal soul.

The exercise can help you move from repetitive thoughts about the incident to a state of peace and grace. You may even reach the point where you thank the person for the opportunity to transform yourself and elevate your consciousness. In a news article, the award-winning English author Emily Koch speaks about a traffic accident in which her legs were broken, "The accident galvanised me to write. It made me realise that life is too short not to do the things that you love." Although angry at first, Koch said, "I've managed to let that anger go. I think if I met him [the driver] now I think I would say thank you. But I'd also tell him to drive more carefully."[3]

The Healing Power of Forgiveness

Two years after my dad died, his spirit returned to the family house and was causing problems for Mum and me. (After Dad's passing, I lived with Mum two or three nights a week to support her.) Mum was aware of Dad's spirit being around her. She would feel him lying beside her in bed. This was disturbing for her as my parents' relationship had been difficult.

My colleague Fotoula, who is psychic, explained to me that Dad's spirit wanted Mum's forgiveness to help him move on in the spirit realms. I then said to Mum that by forgiving Dad, she would release the hurt she held over how he had mistreated her. I told her this would help Dad to move on and also release her from their karmic bond. Else, they would stay attached and have to resolve the situation in another life. Mum understood what I was saying, but was not ready to let go of the pain. Her response was a clear "no." I respected her decision and let the issue go.

A few months after our chat, Mum's world upended. Alone at home, she became disorientated, fell, and in a panic, called the police. (Luckily, she had fallen next to the phone.) The police arrived and called Mum an ambulance. After two weeks in the hospital, Mum was moved to a rehab clinic. After another two weeks, she returned home. I stayed with her for the first two nights. On the third night, I got a call from the personal alarm team saying that Mum had fallen, was disorientated, and was in an ambulance on her way to the hospital. I met her there. Mum stayed in the hospital, again, for two weeks, and again, was moved back to the rehab clinic. By this time, Mum had lost her confidence to live independently, and decided to move into a care home.

All these moves and changes had a profound effect on Mum, especially the second hospital stay. I visited her most days, and sometimes, she would just desperately clutch and kiss my hands. It was heartbreaking to witness, and frightening for her because no doctor could pinpoint the cause of the falls. During many of our visits, we would both break down in tears. Sometimes, she wanted to die. I spoke to her about going into the Light with no regrets, and I thanked her for being my Mum. Her normal reserve fell away, and she shared things about her life that I never knew. It was sad and beautiful at the same time as the love flowed between us.

One day, as we sat outside in the sun at the care home, I asked her if she ever thought about Dad. She turned to me with surprise and said, "No, I never think about him." "Have you forgiven him?" I asked tentatively. She said, "Oh yes. He's out of my life now." She had released all her hurt and anger. In one year, she had had to surrender to so much—the loss of her home, way of life, possessions, and independence. She told me that she now fully accepted her life in the care home and had chosen to live. This was her new home. She felt safe, and the other residents were her family. She liked the staff and knew they would take care of her. She had settled in and was at peace, and it was lovely to see. What a change from the woman who clung desperately to my hands in the hospital. I am so proud of how Mum, then eighty-four, grew. When I look at her now, all I see is a luminous soul with a radiant smile. We are never too old to change. Life will continuously give us opportunities to grow and rebalance our karma.

About two weeks later, Fotoula was leading a guided meditation during a workshop that we were co-teaching. She said that we may see people in front of us, some of whom we may know. The people had come in spirit form to receive the loving energy from our practice. In my mind's eye, as I looked at the sea of faces in front of me, I saw Dad standing at the back between two angels. He looked well, younger than I had ever known him. He waved and in my mind, I saw myself waving back. Then he turned and walked away. He too had transformed. This is the power of forgiveness to heal us in life and death.

Self-Realisation: Living a Meaningful Life

Who are we without the safety net of the conditioned life and identity we have built around us? Who are we without our home, our job, our way of life, our possessions? When one, some, or all of these things are suddenly stripped away from us, as was the case with my mum, how many of us would weather the storm and come out on the other side in a good frame of mind, determined to live and not give up?

The first time that I was made redundant from work, I was shattered. Work was a huge part of my identity. In the space of ten minutes one Friday morning, my foundation was rocked. I stepped into a supermarket soon afterwards and was overwhelmed by feelings of worthlessness. Being unemployed meant that I had no meaningful place in society. I had to get out of the shop as quickly as possible. Picking ourselves up from these events with compassion and forgiveness can support us to find meaning in our life beyond our identity of who we think we are.

Alongside our inner purpose, we each have a life purpose for our current incarnation, which Eckhart Tolle calls our "outer purpose."[4] Finding and living our outer purpose is crucial for our health and happiness. When we are living in alignment with our outer purpose, we invite passion, aliveness, and joy into our life. We are also in sync with our inner purpose.

How do we discover what we are here to do? By following our heart. It is through the connection with our sacred heart that we can actualise our life purpose; otherwise, we are in our mind and in our ego. Some of us may have been lucky to align with our outer purpose naturally as we grew up. For others, life may have intervened and set us on a different course from the one we believed was ours.

Growing up, my dad wanted to be a farmer, influenced by his uncle John, his hero, who worked on a farm in the Scottish Borders. Every summer, Dad spent his school holidays helping Uncle John on the farm. The summer before Dad was due to move and live and work on the farm, Uncle John died. A teacher hearing this news suggested to my dad that he take up a job that allowed him to work with wood as he could see my dad had a natural talent for woodwork. For the rest of his life, Dad worked with wood in various ways, and it brought him and the recipients of his work, joy. Life had interceded to set him in a different direction from the one he expected.

Those of us who never discover what we are here to do can feel unfulfilled and empty, and lack motivation. This was how I felt. When I decided to walk my heart's path, I was led to my outer purpose. When we connect with our sacred heart and follow its guidance, we reignite the fire within us, the Divine spark. This is the aspect of us that knows why we are here and what we are here to do.

Chapter 22

Stepping into the Flow

Doubts arise because of the absence of surrender.[1]
—Sri Ramana Maharshi, Indian sage

In a dream, I see my mind-sets as a precious coin in my hand. Afraid that I might drop the coin, my grip tightens. Despite the pain of the coin digging into my hand, I am too frightened to loosen my grip. Then a voice asks me, "What would you do without the coin? Who would you be without it?" The dream changes course. I see my hand relaxing and my palm opening. The coin remains in my hand without the need to grasp it. I toss the coin into the air, and a sense of freedom sweeps over my whole being. I am free of something that I thought was important. The coin falls back into my hand. But it feels different now. Being free of the coin has changed me. I know I can toss the coin again, and I do, this time a little higher. Again, I taste the freedom of letting go. I start tossing and catching the coin, and each time the coin returns, it is smaller and lighter. I am also different—less fearful and anxious, softer and kinder in my movements and attitudes.

More accepting. The coin is a gift, helping me grow. Just before I wake up, I see myself tossing the coin once again. Did it return? I don't know.

Flowing into Happiness

Usually, when I returned from an overseas trip, I started unpacking immediately, but did not finish. At some point, I would get weary with the unpacking, give up, and do something else. My suitcase would remain in the hall for a few days. Then in 2013, I came back from a trip and my tact changed. I did not automatically start unpacking my suitcase. Instead whatever my attention focussed on—opening the mail, answering emails, cooking dinner, even emptying my suitcase, I did. I moved from one task to another seamlessly. I did not procrastinate, I did not force, I did not think. And, I never became disheartened. I was happy. That night before I went to bed, I had unpacked my suitcase and put everything away, done several clothes washings, looked at all my mail, and completed several other chores—all in one continuous flow of movement.

The concept of flow was recognised in the scientific research of Hungarian-American psychologist Mihaly Csikszentmihalyi.[2] He identified flow as a highly productive mental state of complete absorption that engenders happiness, which affirmed my experience.

This flow moved organically into other areas of my life, such as when I prepare to leave the house each morning. Intuitively, I was shifting from the mind's approach of thinking and planning, to the authentic Self's way, of being and doing. Occasionally, my mind would panic and jerk me back. "What day is it? Where should I be? What do I need? Where am I going?" I answer the questions and continue in the flow.

Awakening, a Journey of Surrender

Going with the flow does not mean giving up our goals; it means surrendering to what life is offering us in each moment. We surrender to what is.

In the present moment, we access our
inner wisdom and allow it to direct our actions.

Surrendering is like dying a conscious death. We die to what no longer supports our growth, our ego self, so that we can birth a new approach led by our wise Self. Surrendering means relinquishing our beliefs and choosing, with awareness, to action our sacred heart's choices. For it is our sacred heart that is in flow with life. We turn away from resistance towards acceptance, from pride towards humility, and from fear towards trust. In surrendering, illusion gives way to truth.

Surrendering can be difficult for the mind to comprehend; it can feel like capitulation. Yet, often we only get what we want when we let go of any desired outcome. How can you let go of wanting something without turning away from your dreams? What if you could hold a wish in your heart rather than in the mind? It is like asking a question without looking for an answer. Let the question weave the magic. As above, in my dream, "Did the coin return?" Let life work out the how of your wish.

When I was in my twenties, I was captivated by a television programme about rafting in the Grand Canyon. I did some research and was drawn to a two-week rafting trip with a two-year waiting list. The reality of planning the trip overwhelmed me, and I put the dream on hold.

Thirty years later, in 2012, I was in America with a friend. Our intention was to fly to San Francisco, drive to Mount Shasta, and then head to Canyon de Chelly National Monument, before flying home from Phoenix. Our plans changed, and we drove from Mount Shasta to the Grand Canyon. In a local shop in Williams, we booked a helicopter tour over the canyon for that afternoon. Then my friend, who was keen to go down to the river, asked the agent about other tours. He mentioned a one-day white water rafting trip. I was spellbound. I told her it was one of my dreams. Well, she said, if this is your dream, we have to do it.

The rafting trip was amazing and frightening; the water was freezing. Within minutes, we were soaked and cold. At one point, on a grade eight rapid, we hit a huge wave. The outboard engine died, and four people, including my friend, were thrown into the middle of the boat. The boat spun around in the crest of the rapid and crashed into some rocks demolishing the outboard motor. Our raft was the only one with a spare outboard, which the boatman managed to start just before the raft was pulled into the next rapid. That day, my prayer for Divine intervention was answered. After the ordeal, my friend turned to me with a look of trepidation, "Do you have any other dreams I should know about?"

Synchronicities and Chance Encounters

Being in the flow brings us into the present moment. In flow, we align with the power of the here and now, and that is when synchronicities, chance encounters, and coincidences happen more often. Seemingly out of the blue, we meet people and situations that either help us move forward in our life's path or complete something from our past. I step out of the café at the exact moment a colleague is passing. I realise the encounter was important for him because he speaks about it at a seminar we both attend a few weeks later. Bill's friend gives him a rattle and suggests they sign up for a weekend workshop on shamanism. Bill reluctantly agrees, and then discovers he loves shamanism and eventually becomes a shamanic teacher. As she experienced her first massage, Evelyn thought how lovely it would be as a job. After the appointment, she meets an acquaintance who told her she was now a massage therapist and where she had trained. Evelyn knows she has to phone the college and enrol in the course.

One day in 2013, I went into the bathroom for a shower. I turned on the taps, but no water came out. I tried the other taps in the house, and no water. Wondering if there was a problem in the street or only in my flat, I knocked on all the other doors in the block of flats. Only one person was home. As the man opened the door, we stared at each other in surprise.

I had first met Alec in 2005, when I worked in a community project in Glasgow's Southside. Alec and I worked well together even although he had frequent disputes with other colleagues. Then two weeks before he left the job, Alec started arguing with me about everything we did. One of my other colleagues advised me to step away. "At some point, this is what happens with everyone who works with Alec," she said, "Now it's your turn." I was hurt and confused by his attitude and refusal to discuss it, but I let it go and then he left. Now, eight years later, we were face-to-face, neither of us had been aware that we were neighbours.

We greeted each other like old friends. Alec checked the taps in his flat and they were working. I thanked Alec and went back to my flat, turned on the taps, and the water flowed. Two weeks later, I was cleaning the bin area at the back of the flats and Alec came out and helped me. We worked together happily chatting for an hour as if nothing had ever happened to strain our relationship. We finished, thanked each other, and went back to our respective flats. A week later, I discovered Alec had moved and I never saw him again. Had life orchestrated the meeting so that any emotional or mental residue from our previous interaction could be resolved?

Trust shows the way[3] —Hildegard of Bingen

Do we trust ourselves to walk our life's path, or let our mind-sets continue to rule?

Shiva is one of the principal deities in Hinduism. In the spirit realms, Shiva is an enlightened being, but when he arrives on Earth, he forgets who he is. Sampling the beautiful food and the pleasures of life, Shiva loses track of his original nature. At some point, he realises the emptiness inside can no longer be filled by life's amusements. Like many spiritual seekers before him, Shiva decides to become a pilgrim and leave behind all the comforts of his everyday life to seek the Divine connection. All he has is an alms bowl, trusting that people will provide food for him to eat and a bed to sleep in, and if not, that life will look after him. In the course of his travels, Shiva finds that he is continually supported.

Shiva wanders through forests and climbs mountains seeking the Divine connection, with trust as his faithful companion. He comes to the white snowcapped mountains as the sun's rays bounce off the snow and reflect light onto him. Shiva wonders, "Am I the mountain, or am I the sun? Am I the ray of light, or am I the whiteness of snow? What am I?" Shiva realises that he is none of these things, and at the same time, he is everything. In that moment, Shiva awakens.

#

I am sitting in a circle of people in the Inyo Mountains in California. We are on a monthlong vision fast guide training with the School of Lost Borders. The trainers tell us that ceremony is at the heart of the vision fast. They give another clear message: trust the ceremony, for it will work in ways your mind cannot imagine. Trust the ceremony. Trust nature. Trust life. Trust yourself. Trust. The path of the heart is about regaining our self-trust.

Self-trust is about learning to listen and action what your inner guidance, your inner wisdom, is advocating. When you do and things work out, trust shows you that something within you is wise and has your best interests at heart.

Solitude and Silence, the Place to Meet Yourself

Austro-German poet Rainer Maria Rilke writes, "All creation holds its breath, listening within me, because, to hear you, I keep silent."[4]

It's the middle of the night and I'm asleep in a single bed in a small, shieling hut. I am on a solitary retreat for the next two weeks. Suddenly, I wake up and look out the window. Perched on a branch is an owl looking directly at me. We hold each other's gaze for a while, and then, silently, the owl turns its head and flies away.

We humans often avoid stillness. The mind fills our days with busyness and disrupts our efforts to stop, sit, and do nothing. Yet, in our core is stillness. This is why solitude and silence can offer us immeasurable gifts if we are prepared to encounter them.

For thousands of years, mystics and contemplatives have retreated from the world. Alone or in small dedicated communities, they meditate, pray, contemplate, and commune with life. They do so not to run away from life but paradoxically to communicate intimately with it, to deepen their experience and understanding of their Divine essence and the interconnectedness of all life. They become wiser, kinder, and more heartfelt human beings. Solitude and silence offer you the opportunity to meet life in a more vibrant, informed way.

Exercise 12. Meeting Yourself in the Silence of the Heart

To help you relax and quieten your mind so that you can meet yourself.

1. Gently close your eyes, and intend to bring all your energy into the body.

2. Imagine you are in a beautiful place in nature. Feel the warmth of the air around you. See the azure blue of the sky and the vibrant colours of nature. Smell the perfume of the flowers. Hear the sound of the river close by.

3. Bring your focus into your heart centre. Imagine you are breathing directly into your heart, and exhaling directly out of your heart. Visualise your heart centre opening.

4. Intend: Breathing in, I open my heart. Breathing out, I relax and surrender. Between the breaths, I pause.

5. Continue breathing in this way as you sit in the silence of the heart for fifteen minutes.

Chapter 23

Embodying Divine Power, Wisdom, and Love

The energy healer is helping me release the pain that has manifested in my solar plexus. I feel emotional. I sense the pain is connected to ancestral patterns around issues of lack and of not deserving comfort and ease in life. As the session progresses, I feel the heaviness leave me, and a feeling of lightness emerges. At the end, the practitioner tells me that the helping spirits are suggesting that I bring the element of fire into my life to burn through my millstone.

"You deserve goodness. You deserve to be comfortable in your life and to have more than enough to live with ease," says the practitioner, "Can you accept this goodness?"

"Yes," I say.

At home, I relax in a hot bath and allow the healing to integrate. The Hindu deity Shiva appears in my awareness. Shiva, the destroyer, transforms through the element of fire. A realisation arises: "It is time to step fully into my power."

#

Much of the journey of awakening is about reclaiming our personal power, the life force that we have ceded consciously and unconsciously through life's experiences. Awakening transforms the base materials, unskillful thoughts and actions, suppressed hurts, and conditioned biology—into gold, our Divine light. This is the path of the spiritual alchemist.

Manifesting Our Divinity

In my weekly meditation circle, we regularly chant the Guru Rinpoche mantra. Guru Rinpoche, or Padmasambhava, is a fully realised spiritual master and the founder of Tibetan Buddhism. Guru Rinpoche is also the subject of many myths. He is known as the one who is "lotus born," reborn into the heart. The lotus is a symbol of awakening and of unconditional love and wisdom. To be lotus born, hence, means to awaken into the enlightened state.

The Guru Rinpoche mantra (in Sanskrit, "Om ah hung vajra guru padma siddhi hung") is a chant of manifestation. We recite it in our circle to manifest our Divine power, represented by the vajra, the diamond and the thunderbolt that can cut through all obstacles. And our Divine wisdom and love, represented by padma, the lotus. These enlightened qualities represent, to me, the Divine masculine (vajra) and the Divine feminine (padma) aspects within us. The masculine power purifies and actions our awareness, so that we can experience the essential Divine feminine state of unconditional love and wisdom.

As your personal work continues and you reclaim more of your Divine power, you strengthen the bridge to the Divine Self. This blossoming inner foundation of power helps sustain your transformational work, while the deepening inner connection to love nourishes and inspires you onwards towards peace and joy.

Harnessing the Power of Intention

In 2009, pre-Peru, as part of my preparations for my first vision quest in the Swiss mountains, I was invited to write a letter of intent for the ceremony.

In every subsequent ceremony and ritual, I have been asked the same question by the facilitators: "What is your intention?" Answering taught me the value of intention. And I have brought intention into all that I do. "What is my intention for this new day (or this meditation practice, or time with Mum, or for my life)?"

By setting an intention, we harness an important universal force, the power of our soul beyond the willpower of the mind.[1] However, our intention can also support our willpower and align it with our soul's wish. In this way, we access the power of our soul and the power of the mind to create the future in accord with our authentic Self.

Intention engages us in a situation, be it a ceremony, a business meeting, or a new day, in a more conscious way. It is a galvanising force. It asks us to be present, to connect within, to be honest and sincere, so that we can be a cocreator with life. Intention is also a statement of self-responsibility. Intention lifts us out of the victim mentality and lower vibrational thinking of the ego mind and empowers us to seek and act on our truth.

This was the power I utilised to find a way to heal the hyperthyroidism (chapter 13). My intention to heal was so strong that, in hindsight, I can see how life brought me the situations and people I needed in order to recover successfully.

Life responds to your intention.

It is crucial to use its power for our highest good. If we use it for anything else, we will, in time, create chaos.

The Awakening of the Spiritual Warrior

A prophecy in ancient Egypt foretold that humanity would fall into darkness. By engaging with the forces of chaos, created by the egoic mind, people would lose their Divine connection. In time, people would then stand up and reclaim their power and their heart. A time of transition, of awakening, would emerge, represented by the spiritual warrior Horus. This would give rise to the time of the heart, another golden era, represented by Osiris.[2] This is the journey of the soul on Earth, individually and collectively.

Enlightened spirit teachers say that we are in the time of Horus, of transition from darkness to light and the awakening of the Divine heart. Times of transition are auspicious for two reasons. One, the energy of change can create deep healing at an individual soul level, the healing of many lifetimes and ancestral healing, as well as in the collective. Two, there is an acceleration in the process of change. This, they say, is why many of us are here on Earth at this time. Our souls wish to experience this time of transition to evolve, purify, and awaken.

As you do the spiritual and personal work and raise your vibration, the energy you send out manifests quicker in your life. It is prudent to be aware: are you sending out gratitude? Or, anger and fear? What you send out is what will be returned to you. What do you want to receive back?

In transitioning times, unexpected events, such as the COVID-19 virus, can transpire. During these challenges, as in any life situation, you have a choice. You can go into the generated collective fear and become anxious. Or, you can engage your awareness, use your strategies for detaching from any unhealthy mind-sets, and continue your spiritual practice to create positivity and access a higher vibrational reality. Can you stay steady in the storm?

The key is to remain centred and stable, connected to your inner light and wisdom, your inner foundation. You become the eye of the storm, the spiritual warrior. The time of transition is asking you to go deeper into your heart and offer compassion to yourself and all who are caught in the whirlwinds. You acknowledge and respect what has to be done at a practical level, while staying positive and connected to the power and light within yourself. In this way you grasp and hold firmly the branch of love, and let go of all the others.

Serving the Highest Good of All

In Buddhism it is usual to dedicate the spiritual practice and ceremonial work to the highest good of all beings, including ourselves. This is known as the dedication of merit practice.[3] The intention is for the merits from the practice to be shared with everyone, especially those who may not be able to have a spiritual practice due to their life circumstances. In this way, we recognise the interconnectedness of all life, and we support the all that we are part of.

For example, at the end of my spiritual practice I place my hands in prayer position on my third eye and say, "I dedicate this practice to the highest good and enlightenment of all beings. May we all awaken into the light that we are, the living light." I then bring my hands, still in prayer position, down to my throat centre and then my heart. In this way I am also asking that what Buddhism calls the three doors—body (third eye, actions), speech (throat, communication), and mind (heart, thoughts)—through which I interact with the world, may be aligned with the highest good of the all.[4]

When I first dedicated my practice in this way, I had no connection with its meaning. It was a ritual at the end of my meditation, nothing more. Gradually, through the repetition and deepening of my practice, I came to understand and experience the importance of the dedication. Now, in meditation, I can feel the interconnectedness I have with all and I know that in supporting my Self for my highest good, I am helping all beings.

One time sitting with my counselling teacher Jane, I listened as she spoke about a life of service, about serving the we rather than the me. Her words stayed with me, and over the years, I often reflected on them. Then one day, a knowingness arose within me and I understood it is the we who is authentic. "The best teacher lodges an intent not in the mind but in the heart,"[5] said novelist Anne Michaels. Jane was such a teacher for me.

Now, each morning before I get out of bed, I say a prayer. I give thanks for the new day and I wish myself the most beautiful of days. I welcome into my life my spirit guides of the Light. I ask for their continued support, and I dedicate the day to be in service to the Light and to the highest good of all. In my heart, I know this is the best gift I can offer my Self, the Earth, and the all.

Interconnectedness

"When we try to pick out anything by itself, we find it hitched to everything else in the Universe,"[6] wrote the Scottish-American explorer, mountaineer, conservationist, and writer John Muir. In other words, in taking care and thinking about the all, we take care of ourselves. In authentically loving ourselves, we look after the collective.

I am standing at a pedestrian crossing. When I press the button, cars and busses will stop, allowing me to cross the road. In that one small action, I will have impacted the lives of all the people in those vehicles. In this way, I see the interconnectedness of life. I wonder in what ways my actions, minor and significant, affect others, and ways other people's behaviour affect my life. Disconnection is a fabrication.

When I was in the Inyo Mountains (chapter 22), I sat with my back against a tree for ninety minutes. At some point, it was as if our energy bodies, our auras, merged. I could no longer feel where my body ended and the tree began. From that place of oneness with the tree, a bigger awareness and connection opened up in me. I could feel a connection with all life.

Ancient and indigenous cultures speak of the "web of life," the energy lines that connect all life on Earth and beyond. The natural world is linked to this web all the time. We echo nature, and the more intimate we become with that echo, the stronger our Divine heart and sense of interconnection grows.

Exercise 13. Experiencing Interconnection

This visualisation uses a tranquil lake as a metaphor for the awakened state to engage with the state of Oneness.

1. Sit quietly for a few minutes. Focus on your breathing as you intend to quieten your mind.

2. Imagine you are standing in front of a lake. The water is still. The subtle, fragrant aroma of lotus flowers fills the air. Clouds in the sky cover the sun, and a mist falls over the lake. Even though the scene is peaceful, you feel that the mist diminishes your experience.

3. Standing with you, around the lake, are all the beings who have ever existed, in the past, present, and future. As you all hold hands, you realise there is only one lake.

4. See yourself and everyone else as the one sun radiating light onto the mist. As the light of everyone's heart shines out the mist dissolves.

5. Watch the mist evaporate through the power of the light. Now you can see the whole lake, the dragonflies and the lotus flowers. Look into the crystal clear water and extend your hand into the water. You are one with everything.

6. Meditate in this space for fifteen minutes.

The peaceful lake always exists. The mist represents the beliefs that obscure the experience of the lake. The sunlight is the spiritual practice that gradually burns away the mist until all there is, is the beauty and tranquility of the lake, the awakened state.

#

Coming home, awakening, is an experiential journey of gradually becoming and embodying our divinity. Not an intellectual journey, awakening is a process of diving ever deeper inside to uncover our true Self issue by issue, cell by cell, truth by truth. We let go of the need to know and step into the unknown. We let go of expectations and surrender to whatever comes.

Awakening is a path in which we walk at the pace that accords with our soul. Each person's path is unique, which is why we cannot compare our progress with someone else's. Each path twists and turns and surprises.

In the road to awakening, we bring the focus back into ourselves. We make our own candle and kindle our inner flame. We accept the help of teachers who appear along the way, knowing we are in charge of our own process. We set our ego mind aside and learn to recognise and follow the voice of our heart. We commit to our path, whatever it may be. We connect with the living light within, until one day we become that light. This is where the path will eventually lead us all, no matter how long, arduous, or smooth the road may be, no matter how many lifetimes it takes.

Chapter 24

Awakening Through the Stillness

Don't challenge yourself to be brave or fearless, challenge yourself to be open and to trust in the higher Self, challenge yourself to remain inwardly still and centered inside your own Being.[1]
—Mooji, Jamaican spiritual teacher

It's May 2019. I only have enough money in the bank to pay my rent and my expenses for June. For the past five years, I have worked without receiving a salary for the ISIS School of Holistic Health. My mum and a friend who have supported me financially for the past two years, can no longer help. My mind, anxious and frightened, says, "Maybe it's time to get a proper job, Fi."

In contrast to my mind's apprehension, my body and heart are calm. The only word I hear is "trust." I have followed this voice since 2007, at age fifty, and it has carried me over so many hurdles. Can I surrender through this new wave of doubt? I acknowledge and meet the feelings of fear and abandonment generated by the nonpaying job and the loss of my two supporters. I know my mind is only trying to protect me by offering solutions. The frightened part of me wonders, "Am I crazy?" "Is it time to concede defeat and find a paying job?" How can my heart be so still and quiet, amid so much doubt? "Trust," I hear again, and, "Stay steady. Stay centred. Continue with your spiritual practices. Let life bring the solution."

Before a two-day course, in sacred space and in front of two friends as witnesses, I state my intention to release all of the self-sabotaging behaviours and attitudes that keep me small. I pledge to accept abundance into my life.

I remain steady. I stay centred. I continue to devote my days to my spiritual practice. I do not let the doubts distract me. Then a miracle happens. Out of the blue, a stranger gives me money for my July expenses. As each successive month takes me to the brink of debt, the situation is resolved by money unexpectedly coming into the School, to fund a salary for me. My wise Self understands this challenge is asking me to release my remaining deep-seated fears and scepticism. Finally, in December 2019, my mind is quiet. Like my heart, my mind knows I will be fine. I have a paid job with the ISIS School!

When Spiritual Practice and Life Merge

Many of the things that I have read in spiritual books and heard in seminars over the years about the awakening process I am now experiencing. The first book I read *The Miracle of Mindfulness*[2] speaks about how everyday tasks, such as washing the dishes, can become part of our self-awareness practice by bringing our focus into the present moment. Now, I am living this experience as I go through my day. My spiritual practice and my everyday life have merged. My whole life is the practice. Increasingly, my attention is focused solely on what I am doing in the moment. When I write an email, I am fully engaged in the writing. Then in flow, guided by my inner wisdom and without thinking, my focus shifts effortlessly to the next thing to be done.

In this state, everything that comes into my awareness to be actioned, is actioned, even small things (such as wiping the refrigerator door handle) that in the past I would have ignored or forgotten, have their place. This new focused attention organically creates balance in my life and allows the movement to continue.

When random thoughts interrupt the flow, I notice my hesitancy, the disruption of the connected state. Karma manifests in this state of disconnection—even with seemingly inconsequential things. (When we are disconnected, we are in our ego mind and our egoic reactions, big and small, will create karma.) One evening, I felt proud of myself for remembering to put my iPod in my handbag for a course I was cofacilitating the following day. It was a fleeting awareness of pride that I did not pay attention to. The next morning, noticing how many things I had to carry, I chose to take my backpack rather than my handbag and left my iPod at home. I knew that the moment of pride had created negative karma that led me to forget the iPod. This is how quickly and subtlety karma can manifest, and especially as our vibration increases. The higher our vibration, the quicker the consequences of our actions return.

Although in most instances, I can now readily action my inner guidance, some situations still trigger resistance.

For weeks, my instinct was to stop watching films and DVDs, yet I ignored it. Films were one of my great loves, my entertainment of choice and preferred way to relax. In December 2018, I bought a DVD box set to watch over Christmas as a treat. After five minutes, the first disk stopped playing. I ejected it, restarted the computer, and watched the next fifteen minutes of the episode before the disk stopped again. After two days of this, I decided to buy a new DVD player. The same thing happened. The disks would not play straight through. Despite the frustration, I persevered, restarting the computer every fifteen minutes. After watching the final episode, I surrendered to the inner guidance and let go of my stubbornness. I cancelled the DVD rental subscription, and stopped buying box sets.

Now when I even think about going to see a film, something else transpires for me to do instead. This is part of an organic renunciation process that has been happening for some years where things that no longer resonate with my vibration are systematically taken away, for example, the television in 2004 and alcohol in 2010.

As my awareness increases, more clarity and understanding present, and with that, comes greater responsibility. Life shows me how important it is to be careful with my actions and words, and I am aware that I am in another learning phase. I apologise to the friend I hurt with a thoughtless remark. She accepts my apology, and is aware of a different teaching for her in the same incident: to hold her truth. From this small lesson, I recognise that in the bigger picture, we are all each other's teachers.

The growth in awareness is happening because my mind has quieted. The personal work and spiritual practices have transformed a large part of the ego mind and only a small part of it still operates, still holds on. In a spiritual practice in 2019, I am shown this clearly. As I chant a mantra, I become aware of my whole being gradually becoming one with the chanting. My voice changes, deepens, and its vibration resonates within me and out into the room. I am absorbed in the energy of the chanting. My mind is trying to pull me back from this connection, not wanting me to fully let go. I sense its fear. "You need me or you'll forget the words," my mind says, even though I have been happily singing the chant. This is the egoic part that is still to be integrated.

The wise part steps back to accommodate the frightened part and not overwhelm it. I am aware of the gift to see the wise part and the conditioned part operating within me and discern what each manifests. All this is happening as I continue to chant. Then, again, I feel the wise part slowly come to the fore, bathe my whole being including the frightened part with its light until I am immersed into the mantra once more. I return to the state of Oneness.

Evidence of Your Soul Evolution

You know you have evolved spiritually when you can overcome issues that in the past would have consumed you for days, months, even years, much quicker; let go, especially if you let go of something that was precious to you or touched your heart; and view each day as a new adventure without fear or worry of what may happen. With each of these markers, you are moving into the state of the observer, the state of the awakened mind.

The Higher Self and Divine Union

Wise spirit teachers say that there is an aspect of ourselves that never incarnates, that always remains in the spirit realms. This aspect is called the "higher Self" (HS).

*The higher Self is the expansiveness of
our spiritual being, the awakened consciousness.*

Your spiritual development on Earth is governed by your HS. Your HS has set the path for your incarnated soul to walk and, at some point, to awaken through this experience. As the incarnated soul carries the higher spirit essence, the soul can recognise and choose to follow its predestined spiritual path. As you progress on your spiritual journey and your soul's vibration increases, the relationship between the soul and the HS becomes stronger. These two aspects of yourself connect and communicate, especially when you do spiritual practices. During such times, you may receive a download of energy from the HS, that helps your Earth soul heal the separation between the mind and heart. (The HS is never separate from the incarnated soul, but in this illusionary world, the soul on Earth can feel isolated and rudderless.) This union energises and strengthens you to walk your soul's path and open your heart further towards the living light of your essential nature.

With each union, you experience your Divine light to the extent you are able at the time. As these unions become more frequent, a truer resonance emanates from you. You move deeper within, embody more of your light, stay steadier in the awakening process, and with what is happening in the outside world. This bond brings you strength, inner knowing, and insights, and deepens your connection with Self and all life. This helps you detach further from your ego mind since it weakens the conditioned attachments within you. You are birthing into Oneness that will occur many times until you awaken fully.

In a shamanic journey, I see a heron bird gliding gracefully, its huge wings extended, negotiating the air currents effortlessly. The scene changes. The heron is standing in shallow water, still and completely focused. Suddenly, its head darts forward into the water and emerges with a fish in its beak. The heron eats the fish and resumes its still pose. The heron is a teaching from the HS, showing me how to live life. There is no flapping, no unnecessary movement, only assuredness and ease.

The Beauty of Life is in the Current Moment

As the unions with my HS progress, I am able to spend longer in the higher states of consciousness. The stillness within, created by the transformation of the ego state, gradually expands, and opens doors in my heart to other levels of awareness. My concentration and focus strengthen and become a powerful force for change. I am aware of my authentic power growing from within, and I remain steady despite the changes that are taking place in my immediate circumstances (cancelling of workshops) and in the world events around me, due to the COVID-19 pandemic.

Looking in the mirror, I see how all the changes within me are reflected in my eyes—clarity, stillness, self-assuredness—like the heron. I hardly recognise the person looking back. "Who are you?" I wonder. "Who is being birthed?"

Exercise 14. A Spiritual Practice of the Living Light

This practice is offered as a way to strengthen your energy body and increase your vibration.

1. Sit for a few minutes with your attention focussed in your heart centre.

2. Using each of your senses, become aware of the beauty that exists around you. Extend gratitude to Mother Nature for all her manifestations.

3. Acknowledge the beauty that exists in your life, the sequence of events that have brought you to this moment. Recognise all that life has given you and how it has supported you in your earthly experience. Give thanks for all you have and for your life.

4. Sense the beauty of your body. Every aspect of your body is made in alignment with Divine order to express your soul's wishes. Offer appreciation for your body as it allows you to experience physical life in your own way.

5. Observe the beauty that lies within your sacred heart. Give thanks for the light that you are, the living light incarnated in the physical world. In this space of gratitude and awareness, intend to open the door of your heart and allow your light to radiate and expand around you.

6. As you bathe in the light of your sacred heart say, "I merge with the universal light of the world so that I may become this light. May the high vibrational energies of the living light now flow within my sacred heart, for the highest good of all beings." Meditate in this space for a minimum of fifteen minutes.

7. Slowly, come back from the meditation, and gently open your eyes.

Chapter 25

Into the Living Light

Human beings look for security. We seek peace, happiness, and love from those around us. What we seek outside of us, we already have inside. The brilliance of your spirit is love. Everything you seek outside is transitory and when you attach emotionally to it, you will eventually grieve its loss. Witness the changes in your own body. It is the same with your world, it continues to change in ways that you cannot control. The light of your spirit is constant. No matter what happens to you, it always is.

In connecting with the love of your spirit you develop acceptance of yourself, acceptance of life, and acceptance of the world. You experience the living light of your authentic Self. You come home. As Emaho, Native American shaman, says, "And when one awakens, the winds stop. When one awakens, the storms stop. Life just is."[1]

Four Facets of Awakening

In the journey to awakening four facets of spiritual evolution create a path for us to walk: awareness, initiation, purification, and Divine union.

Awareness. You consciously become the observer, the witness, the one who is aware of their thoughts, feelings, and actions. You see where you cede power and consciously take back your authority. You put your wise Self in charge.

Initiation. Through personal challenges, illness, attunements, ceremonies, rituals, and rites of passage, you may be initiated or birth yourself into higher states of awareness.

Purification. The clearing and healing stage has many layers. Perhaps you have energetic imprints, karma, trauma, and physical conditions from this and other lives and those of your ancestors. Clearing these heavy energies may have a physical effect (nausea, fever, or fatigue), an emotional effect (tears or laughter), and a mental effect (released painful memories). Purification can also take place in your life. Many changes, such as a new job, may occur to bring you back onto your soul's path.

Divine union. You lighten your body and mind through repeated unions with the awakened state that lies within and outside of you. Once experienced, these moments flee and return. And each union can be more profound and stronger than its predecessor, especially if you continue with your spiritual practices and live in accord with your authentic Self. In these merges, all that you are is accepted by the Divine.

The four facets are linked, but the order can differ from person to person, and you may experience them at different times in your life. They are experienced and reexperienced, with each step of each facet paving the way towards a deeper understanding and connection. Trust these phases, even when the mind is frightened or impatient. Continue with your spiritual practice and personal work.

At some point, through all your personal work and practices, when a particular frequency is reached and anchored in the body, you awaken into your Divine light. Your mind, body, spirit and heart are fully integrated and harmonised within. They unite into one single vibration, into Oneness, and the state of separation falls away as if it was never there. Your eyes reflect the new perspective and understanding of the awakened state. Until then, you may continue to have glimpses of this state. You may feel it in different intensities, but not live it. These glimpses, or fleeting experiences, pave the way towards full awakening into the embodiment and presence of the authentic Self.

The Inner and Outer Spirals of Awakening

As we continue to do the personal work we meet ourselves at ever deepening levels of awareness. I call this the inner spiral of awakening. At the same time, our spiritual practices invite us to reach ever higher towards the infinite. This is the outer spiral of awakening.

Consciously attending to our personal issues and committed to our spiritual practice, we are in flow with the movement of these two spirals, which support our soul's evolution. In contrast, when we focus on one area and ignore the other, we create an imbalance and limit our efforts. For example, when we concentrate predominantly on spiritual practice and ignore the personal work to clear the body and address our emotional and behavioural patterns, we cannot ground our spiritual work. We may lose ourselves in a spiritual expression that does not support everyday life. We have not created the space for the body, the container, to hold the higher vibrational energy.

Similarly, when we devote our time to personal work without Divine union, we are cutting ourselves off from a rich and supportive resource, and potentially making our personal growth onerous, spending years trying to heal the same traumas. When we combine both aspects, we can spiral in and go deeper and spiral out and reach higher levels of consciousness. Each supports and balances the other, and paves the way for further openings and clearings.

It is in this light that I continue the journey of awakening. I rise each morning and do my spiritual practice, aware as much as I can be of the issues life is asking me to address or release. Strengthening the connection with the authentic Self within and the higher Self above. Standing stronger in my own power. Continually clearing the body of the heavier energies so the vessel is cleaner and energetically lighter. Watching as events unfold in the world and choosing to stay detached but observant. Increasingly, in the world but not of the world.

Sitting in meditation, October 2019, I consciously engage with my higher Self and feel an expansion of light within. A memory of the Marianne Williamson quote that I used as my intention on my first vision quest in 2009 surfaces, "Our deepest fear is not that we are inadequate. Our deepest fear is that we are powerful beyond measure. It is our Light, not our Darkness, that most frightens us."[2]

I am no longer frightened of my light. I embrace it. "Come home, dear one," my soul says to me. "Yes", I hear myself saying. I become the light that I am.

Afterword: The Gift of Light

During the COVID-19 lockdown in 2020, my mum passed away. It was very quick. I received a call from the care home on Monday, 27 April, to tell me Mum had the virus symptoms. I went to see her that afternoon. Mum could hardly speak. The only two sentences I understood were, "I'm going home," and her last coherent words, "I love you."

On Tuesday, I spent eleven hours at Mum's bedside, speaking to her, chanting mantras, and singing the silly songs we made up on our recent outings. All the while, she was unconscious. On Wednesday, I got the call to tell me Mum had died. I immediately drove to the home to be with her.

The spiritual path I follow, the Path of ISIS, contains practices for helping a soul transition into the spirit realms after death. As I stood beside Mum's body, I created a sacred space in the room and performed the healing practices. When the ritual was complete, I knew Mum's physical body carried no essence of her spirit. Due to the specific mantras I chanted, all of Mum's essence had moved out of her body and into the spirit realm. I felt calm and blessed to offer Mum this healing.

I was then filled with an incredible sense of peace and joy. Unconditional love flowed all around me and instead of sadness, I felt euphoric. This was the gift of Mum's passing. When the spirit door opened and Mum's essence left, the light from the spirit realms flowed into me and I was lifted into a higher state of consciousness.

I rang my colleague Fotoula to tell her what had happened, and she was able to speak with Mum psychically. Mum spoke about the relatives who had met her on the spirit side and said that she had no regrets and that she remembered everything I had said to her the previous day. This was lovely to hear. Mum had been fully aware of her transition into the spirit realm.

If we, the living, are able to accept this transmission of light at the point of someone's passing, we will not feel the sadness of separation and the grief associated with death. A deeper sense of joy and love will become our reality, just as the spiritual teachings of Buddhism and ancient Egypt say.

I have been practising the Path of ISIS for ten years. Through this work, I have generated a higher state of consciousness. As Mum's spirit transitioned, I was aware and steady, and connected to my authentic Self. I fully accepted the situation and received a final gift of grace and light from my beloved Mum's passing.

On reflection, I can see how my spiritual and personal work over many years has enabled me to cope with major issues, such as death, and transcend the conditioned mind-sets. What I experienced in the moment of Mum's final passing, was understanding, grace, and beauty, instead of overwhelming grief. This is the gift of living life with awareness of our spiritual light, that you too can attain.

The more you harness your spiritual nature and live in accord with your authentic Self, the more you will embody your enlightened essence. You will be lifted out of the egoic mind-sets and transcend limiting beliefs.

This higher awareness is now my reality, generated through the near-death experience in Peru and the years of focused spiritual work and personal development. I know with every cell of my being that the higher states of consciousness are accessible and incredibly beautiful. I know this too can be your reality.

Notes

Chapter 1

1. Thomas O. Lambdin, trans. Coptic version, B.P. Grenfell and A. S. Hunt, trans. Greek fragments, Bsentley Layton, trans. Greek fragments, and Craig Schenk, comm., "The Gospel of Thomas," verse 70, https://www.sacred-texts.com/chr/thomas.htm. Accessed on 12 April 2020.

Chapter 2

1. Thich Nhat Hanh, *Peace Is Every Step: The Path of Mindfulness in Everyday Life* (Rider, 1995), 41.

Chapter 3

1. Joseph Campbell, *A Joseph Campbell Companion: Reflections on the Art of Living*, ed. Diane K. Osbon (HarperCollins, 1991), 18.

Chapter 4

1. Edward Young, Edith J. Morley, ed., *Edward Young's Conjectures on Original Composition* (The University Press, Manchester), 2019, 20.
2. Sister Stanislaus Kennedy, *Now Is the Time: Spiritual Reflections* (Town House Dublin, expanded ed. 2006), 16.

Chapter 5

1. Donna Eden and David Feinstein, *Energy Medicine: How to Use Your Body's Energies for Optimum Health and Vitality* (Piatkus, 2008).
2. J. L. Creed and A. E. Wardman, trans., *The Philosophy Of Aristotle*. With an introduction and commentary by Renford Bambrough (Mentor, 1963).

3. Li Zhaoping and Li Jingling, "Filling-In and Suppression of Visual Perception from Context: A Bayesian Account of Perceptual Biases by Contextual Influences," *PLoS Computational Biology* 4(2): e14, 15 February 2008, https://journals.plos.org/ploscompbiol/article?id=10.1371/journal.pcbi.0040014.

Chapter 6

1. Jack Kornfield, *A Path with Heart: A Guide through the Perils and Promises of Spiritual Life* (Rider, rev. and upd. ed. 2002), 276.
2. Eckhart Tolle, *The Power of Now: A Guide to Spiritual Enlightenment* (Hodder & Stoughton, 2005).
3. Stephen Levine and Ondrea Levine, *Who Dies? An Investigation of Conscious Living and Conscious Dying* (Bantam Doubleday Dell Publishing Group, reissue ed. 1989).
4. Robert Burns, *Poems and Songs of Robert Burns,* ed. James Barke (Fontana / Collins, 1960), 138.
5. Ram Dass, *Be Here Now* (Crown Publications, 1971).

Chapter 7

1. Daniel Siegel, *Mindsight: Transform Your Brain with the New Science of Kindness* (Oneworld Publications, 2011).

Chapter 8

1. William Shakespeare, *The Oxford Shakespeare Hamlet*, Oxford World's Classics, ed. G. R. Hibbard (Oxford University Press, reiss. 2008), 2.2: 247-8.
2. C. G. Jung, *The Essential Jung: Selected Writings Introduced by Anthony Storr* (Fontana Press, new ed. 1998).
3. Martin E. P. Seligman and Mihaly Csikszentmihalyi, "Positive Psychology: An Introduction," *American Psychologist, 55,* 5-14, 2000.
4. Herbert Benson, John F. Beary, and Mark P. Carol, "The Relaxation Response," *Journal of Psychiatry: Interpersonal and Biological Processes, 37*(1), 37-46, 1974.
5. Norman Cousins, *Anatomy of an Illness: As Perceived by the Patient* (W. W. Norton & Company, 20th ann. ed. 2005).

Chapter 9

1. Sandra Ingerman, "Medicine for the Earth," 2012, http://www.sandraingerman.com/sandrasarticles/medicinefortheearth.html.
2. T. S. Eliot, author, Christopher Ricks and Jim McCue, eds., *The Poems of T. S. Eliot Volume I: Collected and Uncollected Poems* (Faber & Faber, main ed., 2018) 189.

3. Eric Berne, M. D., *Games People Play: The Psychology of Human Relationships* (Penguin Life, 2016).

Chapter 10

1. John Carlin, https://homeopathy-soh.org/homeopath/john-carlin/
2. Madeleine Black, "Unbroken—Speaking the Unspeakable," 21 June 2019, TEDxGlasgow, https://www.youtube.com/watch?v=_ouhY155398.
3. "How does Transformational Breath work?" Breathwork FAQ, Transformation Breath Foundation, http://www.transformationalbreath. com/breathwork.aspx. Accessed on 19 April 2020.
4. Jill Bolte Taylor, Ph.D., *My Stroke of Insight: A Brain Scientist's Personal Journey* (New American Library, 2009), 146.
5. Ann Weiser Cornell, PhD, *The Power of Focusing: A Practical Guide to Emotional Self-Healing* (New Harbinger, 2002).
6. Gangaji, *The Diamond in Your Pocket: Discovering Your True Radiance* (Cygnus Books, 2005), 138.
7. "Confronting History: James Baldwin," Charmaine Li, https://kinfolk. com/confronting-history-james-baldwin/. Accessed on 19 April 2020.

Chapter 11

1. Pascal Mercier, *Night Train to Lisbon* (Atlantic Books, 2009), 378.
2. Steven Halpern, PhD, *Tuning the Human Instrument: Keeping Yourself in "Sound Health"* (Halpern Sounds, upd. ed. 1980).
3. Lorna Byrne, "An Evening with Lorna Byrne" (Seminar, Glasgow Royal Concert Hall, Glasgow, Scotland, April 6, 2017).

Chapter 12

1. Jiddu Krishnamurti, "Krishnamurti's Journal," https://selfdefinition.org/ krishnamurti/Jiddu_Krishnamurti_Journal(1973-75).pdf, 84. Accessed on 19 April 2020.
2. Gareth S. Hill, *Masculine and Feminine: The Natural Flow of Opposites in the Psyche* (Shambhala, 2001).
3. Betty J. Eadie, *Embraced by the Light: The Most Profound and Complete Near-Death Experience Ever* (Bantam, reprint ed. 2002).

Chapter 13

1. Lisa Feldman Barrett, *How Emotions Are Made: The Secret Life of the Brain* (Houghton Mifflin Harcourt, 2017).
2. Martha G. Welch and Robert J. Ludwig, "Calming Cycle Theory and the Co-Regulation of Oxytocin," *Psychodynamic Psychiatry* 45(4):519–20, 2017, Special Issue: Neurobiology of Attachment.

3. Fotoula Adrimi, *The Golden Book of Wisdom: Ancient Spirituality and Shamanism for Modern Times* (The ISIS School of Holistic Health, 2018).
4. Clinton Ober, Stephen T. Sinatra, MD, and Martin Zucker, *Earthing: The Most Important Health Discovery Ever!* (Basic Health Publications, Inc., 2nd ed. 2014).
5. Ruth Hull, *The Complete Guide to Reflexology* (The Write Idea Ltd., 2011).
6. Peter Deadman and Mazin Al-Khafaji, with Kevin Baker, "A Manual of Acupuncture," http://amanualofacupuncture.com. Accessed on 19 May 2020.
7. David Berceli, PhD, *The Revolutionary Trauma Release Process: Transcend Your Toughest Times* (Namaste Publishing, 2008).
8. Louise L. Hay, *You Can Heal Your Life* (Hay House, Inc., 2007).
9. Eckhart Tolle, *The Power of Now: A Guide to Spiritual Enlightenment* (Hodder & Stoughton, 2005), 29.
10. Mark Twain, The Quotations Page, http://www.quotationspage.com/quote/35955.html. Accessed on 20 April 2020.
11. Marc A. Russo, Danielle M. Santarelli, and Dean O'Rourke (2017), "The Physiological Effects of Slow Breathing in the Healthy Human," *Breathe* 13:298–309, doi:10.1183/20734735.009817.

Chapter 14

1. Marion Woodman, in Bessel A. van der Kolk, *The Body Keeps the Score: Brain, Mind, and Body in the Healing of Trauma* (Penguin, 2015), 230.
2. Debbie Ford, *The Dark Side of the Light Chasers: Reclaiming Your Power, Creativity, Brilliance, and Dreams* (Hodder Paperbacks, 2001).
3. Candace B. Pert, *Everything You Need to Know to Feel Good* (Hay House Publishers, UK ed. 2007).

Chapter 15

1. "Success Stories: Twelve Positive Quotes of Wisdom by Maya Angelou," Simple Capacity, https://simplecapacity.com/2014/06/12-positive-quotes-of-wisdom-by-maya-angelou/. Accessed on 21 April 2020.
2. David R. Hawkins, MD, PhD, *Power vs. Force: The Hidden Determinants of Human Behavior* (Hay House, Inc., 2002), 128.
3. "Neuroscience Reveals: Gratitude Literally Rewires Your Brain to Be Happier," Daily Health Post Editorial, Daily Health Post, 21 July 2019, https://dailyhealthpost.com/gratitude-rewires-brain-happier/?utm_source=facebook&utm_medium=social&utm_campaign=SocialWarfare&fbclid=IwAR1ucMEHH4imQTQLec_fUrMwn5SQopl2GMFlpSzpitxjGPCEohB61HbYam0.

4. Dr Valerie Hunt, *Infinite Mind: Science of the Human Vibrations of Consciousness* (Non Basic Stock Line, 2nd ed. 1996).

Chapter 16

1. "Michelangelo Buonarroti > Quotes > Quotable Quote," goodreads, https://www.goodreads.com/quotes/1191114-the-sculpture-is-already-complete-within-the-marble-block-before. Accessed on 21 April 2020.
2. Elisabeth Haich, *Initiation* (Aurora Press, new ed. 2000).
3. Eckhart Tolle, *A New Earth: Create a Better Life* (Penguin Books, 2009).
4. Dr. Elisabeth Kübler-Ross, Quotes, Elisabeth Kübler-Ross Foundation, https://www.ekrfoundation.org/elisabeth-kubler-ross/quotes/. Accessed 21 April 2020.
5. Osho, *The Fish in the Sea is Not Thirsty* (Wisdom Tree, 2008).
6. Paramahansa Yogananda, *Autobiography of a Yogi* (Self-Realization Fellowship, new ed. 2006).
7. Lyz Cooper, *"Sound Affects: Sound Therapy, Altered States of Consciousness, and Improved Health and Wellbeing,"* 2016, https://www.britishacademyofsoundtherapy.com/wp-content/uploads/2016/01/ASC-research-article-HealthySound.pdf.
8. Alfred A. Tomatis, *The Conscious Ear* (Station Hill Press, 1991).
9. Mitchell L. Gaynor, MD, *The Healing Power of Sound: Recovery from Life-threatening Illness Using Sound, Voice, and Music* (Shambhala Publications Inc., 2002).

Chapter 17

1. Shri Mataji Nirmala Devi, 27 July 1988, "Nirmal Quotes," Sahaja Yoga Centers, New York, NY, https://sycenters.org/quotes/981.
2. Daniel Goleman and Richard J. Davidson, *The Science of Meditation: How to Change Your Brain, Mind, and Body* (Penguin Life, 2018).
3. David S. Black and George M. Slavich, "Mindfulness Meditation and the Immune System: A Systematic Review of Randomized Controlled Trials," *Annals of the New York Academy of Sciences*, 1373(1): 13–24, 2016. https://www.ncbi.nlm.nih.gov/pmc/articles/PMC4940234/.
4. Julie A. Jacob, MA, "As Opioid Prescribing Guidelines Tighten, Mindfulness Meditation Holds Promise for Pain Relief," *Journal of the American Medical Association*, 315(22): 2385–87 2016.
5. Miles McDowell, *Brainwaves: The Nature Of Brain Waves and Their Frequencies—How They Affect You and How You Can Change Them* (e-book, 2015).
6. Evelyn C. Rysdyk with Bhola Nath Banstola, *The Nepalese Shamanic Path: Practices for Negotiating the Spirit World* (Destiny Books, 2019).
7. Elisabeth Haich, *Initiation* (Aurora Press, new ed. 2000).

8. Bessel van der Kolk, *The Body Keeps the Score: Mind, Brain, and Body in the Transformation of Trauma* (Penguin, 1st ed. 2015).

9. Fotoula Adrimi, *The Golden Book of Wisdom: Ancient Spirituality and Shamanism for Modern Times* (The ISIS School of Holistic Health, 2018), 31.

Chapter 18

1. Sandra Ingerman, *Soul Retrieval: Mending the Fragmented Self* (HarperOne, rev. and upd. ed. 2010).

2. Madeleine Black, *Unbroken: Used, Beaten but Never Broken* (John Blake Publishing Ltd, 2017).

3. Bessel van der Kolk, *The Body Keeps the Score: Mind, Brain and Body in the Transformation of Trauma* (Penguin, 1st ed. 2015), 180.

4. Pascal Mercier, *Night Train to Lisbon* (Atlantic Books, 2009), 239.

5. David R. Hawkins, MD, PhD, *Power vs. Force: The Hidden Determinants of Human Behavior* (Hay House, Inc., 2002).

Chapter 19

1. Aletheia Luna, "Seven Types of Spirit Guides (and How to Connect with Them)," Lonerwolf, https://lonerwolf.com/connect-with-spirit-guides/. Accessed on 16 January 2020.

2. William Bloom, *Working With Angels, Fairies And Nature Spirits* (Piatkus, 2002).

Chapter 20

1. Meredith Little Foster, *The School of Lost Borders: A Love Story* (Lost Borders Press, 2018), 21.

2. Fotoula Adrimi, *The Golden Book of Wisdom: Ancient Spirituality and Shamanism for Modern Times* (The ISIS School of Holistic Health, 2018).

3. Harriet Beecher Stowe, *Oldtown Folks* (J.R. Osgood, 1873), 570.

Chapter 21

1. Gangaji, "Top Twenty Gangaji Quotes," https://www.youtube.com/watch?v=4Oij36_WcBY. Accessed on 11 May 2020.

2. Marshall B. Rosenberg, PhD, *Nonviolent Communication—A Language of Life* (Puddle Dancer Press (US), 3rd ed., 2015), 49.

3. "Author Emily Koch: 'I'm not angry at the driver who broke my legs,'" *BBC News*, 8 January 2020, https://www.bbc.co.uk/news/uk-england-bristol-51032231.

4. Eckhart Tolle, *A New Earth: Create a Better Life* (Penguin Books, 2009).

Chapter 22

1. Ramana Maharshi, Arthur Osborne, ed. *The Teachings of Ramana Maharshi* (Rider, 2014), 85.
2. Mihaly Csikszentmihalyi, *Flow: The Classic Work on How to Achieve Happiness* (Rider, new ed. 2002).
3. Hildegard of Bingen, Gabriele Uhlein, author, *Meditations with Hildegard of Bingen* (Bear & Company, orig. ed. 1983), 9.
4. Rainer Maria Rilke, Anita Barrows and Joanna Macy, trans., *Rilke's Book of Hours: Love Poems to God* (Riverhead Books, 100th ann. ed. 2005), 79.

Chapter 23

1. Carlos Castenada, *The Active Side of Infinity* (Harper Perennial, 2000).
2. Jonathan Cott, *Search for Omm Sety: A Story of Eternal Love* (Olympic Marketing Corp., 1987).
3. Thubten Chodron, *Guided Buddhist Meditations: Essential Practices on the Stages of the Path* (Shambhala Publications Inc., 2019).
4. The Dalai Lama, author, Jinpa Geshe Thubten, trans., *The World of Tibetan Buddhism: An Overview of Its Philosophy and Practice* (Wisdom Publications, U.S., 2005).
5. Anne Michaels, *Fugitive Pieces: A Novel* (Bloomsbury Publishing PLC, 2009), 121.
6. John Muir, *John Muir Nature Writings: The Story of My Boyhood and Youth; My First Summer in the Sierra; The Mountains of California; Stickeen* (CreateSpace Independent Publishing Platform, Amazon, 2018), 98.

Chapter 24

1. Mooji, 14 October 2017, https://www.facebook.com/moojiji/posts/dont-challenge-yourself-to-be-brave-or-fearlesschallenge-yourself-to-be-openand-/10155342302903962/.
2. Thich Nhat Hanh, *The Miracle of Mindfulness: A Manual on Meditation* (Beacon Press, rev. ed. 1988).

Chapter 25

1. Emaho, *The Winds of Your Heart* (Sequoyah Publishing, 2005), 254.
2. Marianne Williamson, *A Return to Love: Reflections on the Principles of a Course in Miracles* (Thorsons, revised ed., 1996), 190.

About the Author

Fi Sutherland, BEd (hons.), BSc (psychology), is a teacher in the ISIS School of Holistic Health, a Scotland-based school of healing arts, spiritual development, and inner transformation. *Coming Home: Awakening through the Stillness into the Living Light* is the culmination of Fi's decades-long journey in personal and spiritual development, her education in psychology, clinical observations and experience in counselling, and immersion in ancient and indigenous cultures throughout the world.

Born and raised in a small village outside Glasgow, Fi originally trained as a physical education teacher, and represented both Scotland and New Zealand at international volleyball competitions. In 1982, Fi immigrated to New Zealand, and worked in the graphic design field in Wellington. Returning to Glasgow in 2001, Fi completed university and a three-year, advanced therapeutic counselling diploma. Over the next decade, Fi built her career as a counsellor, energy healer, clinical supervisor, and personal development coach.

When a project closed in 2012, Fi stepped away from regular employment and focussed on her spiritual path. She has made numerous pilgrimages and taken part in trainings, retreats, ceremonies, and soul healings in Nepal and Tibet, Egypt, the United States, Brazil, China, France, Germany, Greece, Scotland, England, and Wales.

Since 2015, Fi has worked alongside ISIS School founder Fotoula Adrimi and cofacilitates courses and retreats in meditation and spiritual and personal development. *Coming Home: Awakening through the Stillness into the Living Light* shares remarkable experiences of struggle and healing, and insights and wisdoms across several modalities. Some of Fi's areas of study are highlighted below.

After an introductory course in spirituality in 1995, Fi's journey with Buddhism began with a meditation course facilitated by the late Navachitta, order member, Friends of the Western Buddhist Order (FWBO), Wellington, New Zealand. For five years, Fi attended the FWBO's meditation evenings, retreats, and puja ceremonies. Fi loved the support of the sangha (spiritual community). Navachitta introduced Fi to works by Thich Nhat Hanh, Zen Buddhist Teacher, Community of Interbeing. Inspired by his writing, Fi attended a five-day retreat led by Thay in St Andrews, Scotland, in 2003.

Fi continued to read widely in Buddhist literature. Joseph Goldstein and Jack Kornfield, cofounders of the Insight Meditation Society in the United States, together with Thay, brought Buddhist psychology and meditation alive for Fi. She felt a huge relief to find this understanding.

When Fi returned to Scotland, in 2001, she attended the weekly meditation circle of the Community of Interbeing in Glasgow. Then in 2005, her late counselling college tutor, Jane Robertson-Reick, gave her a picture of the Native American Shaman Emaho. Fi knew immediately that she wanted to meet him. Over the next decade, Fi attended Emaho's Fire Dance ceremonies throughout Europe. Jane and Emaho taught Fi about the importance of the heart.

During those years, Fi investigated other ways of connecting deeper within. She augmented her own personal counselling with numerous workshops and courses, such as Transformational Breath®, and the Naked Voice workshops of Chloë Goodchild. Through these, Fi learnt how to face and release emotions, work with the shadow side, and gain insights into the body's role in awakening.

Fi has also completed three vision quests and trained as a vision quest facilitator with the School of Lost Borders in California. After years of participating in sweat lodges, in 2011, Fi trained as a water pourer in the Native American Sun Bear tradition. These and other spiritual ceremonies, as well as seven moon dances, Emaho's fire dances, and work with Nepalese Shaman Bhola Nath Banstola, taught Fi about the transformative power of ceremony.

In 2009, Fi worked with native shamans in Peru. As a result of a reaction to the high altitude, she had a near-death experience. This incident and the subsequent healings that Fi received from Fotoula Adrimi changed the direction of her life. She knew she had to learn about the ancient Egyptian spirituality that Fotoula had channelled. In 2010, Fi took her first course in the Teachings of the Living Light / The Path of ISIS. Fi continues to work daily with these teachings and practices that help her open and integrate her mind, body, heart, and spirit, and come home into the living light of her authentic Self.

Further Information

The ISIS School of Holistic Health, offers a rich programme of spiritual teachings in retreats, workshops and practice groups in Scotland, southern Germany and online. The School currently offers six main teachings that aim to help people in their spiritual journey of awakening through the practice of chanting, meditation, group work, shamanic journeying, ceremony, work in nature, and pilgrimages to sacred sites. Programmes include:

The Temple of Gaia: The Teachings of the Living Light / The Path of ISIS

The OSIRIS Ascension Teachings

The Rays of Divine Consciousness

Shamanic Practitioner's Course and workshops

Meditation

The Priestess of the Moon Training

For further information on the courses offered and the School's programme, please visit:
www.theisisschoolofholistichealth.com or www.facebook.com/theisisschoolofholistichealth

Lightning Source UK Ltd.
Milton Keynes UK
UKHW020725250822
407828UK00011B/1498